BIG SAM
and the *Big O*

Recollections and Revelations
From a Lifetime of Bass Fishing and
Luremaking on Lake Okeechobee

Robert U. Montgomery

RUM Publishing

Big Sam and the Big O
Recollections and Revelations From a Lifetime of Bass Fishing and
Luremaking on Lake Okeechobee
Robert U. Montgomery
RUM Publishing

Published by RUM Publishing, Bonne Terre, MO
Copyright ©2020 Robert U. Montgomery
All rights reserved.

Cover and Interior design: Davis Creative, DavisCreative.com

Library of Congress Cataloging-in-Publication Data

Library of Congress Control Number: 2020916659

Robert U. Montgomery

Big Sam and the Big O

Recollections and Revelations From a Lifetime of Bass Fishing and Luremaking on Lake Okeechobee

ISBN: 978-1-7330033-4-6

Library of Congress subject headings:

1. BIO000000 Biography & Autobiography / General   2. SPO014000 Sports & Recreation / Fishing   3. NAT018000   Nature/ Ecosystems & Habitats / Lakes, Ponds & Swamps

2020

This book is a tribute to Sam Griffin, the Man, the Myth, the Legend, and my longtime friend. Additionally, I dedicate it to his wife, Carol, who provided invaluable assistance and to all those who contributed stories and memories of how Sam has enriched their lives. Finally, this book is for Cougie too.

Contents

Introduction

This book is about two American treasures.

Mostly it is about my friend, Sam Griffin, a legendary fishing guide and luremaker who was inducted into the National Fresh Water Fishing Hall of Fame in 2019.

But by extension, it also is about Lake Okeechobee, one of the nation's premiere bass fisheries. Sailors talk about the sea being their mistress. For Big Sam Griffin, it is the Big O.

Sam was born and grew up on its waters. As an adult, he has spent thousands of hours there, field-testing his wooden baits, guiding clients, and catching the lake's "little green creatures." All the while, too, he has studied his mistress, her moods, her peculiarities, and, sadly in recent years, her declining health. Arguably, no one knows the Big O as well as Big Sam.

Part I, *Life on the Lake*, provides a look into Sam's formative years, growing up on the lake, helping out his father Joe with commercial fishing—as only a rambunctious young boy can—and, later, at Uncle Joe's Fish Camp. It reveals how he transitioned into the lure business. And it provides a look at the lake and its fisheries and how they changed as Sam grew to adulthood. You might be surprised to learn what Sam thinks about hydrilla on Lake Okeechobee, an invasive aquatic plant much prized by most anglers.

Part II, *Baits and Bass*, examines his handmade lures and reveals the fish-catching expertise that he has shared with me over the years, especially with wooden topwaters, his specialty. As with the Big O, arguably no one knows as much about topwater fishing as he does.

Part III, *The Man, the Myth, the Legend*, takes a look at the life of Sam Griffin, as related by relatives and friends, including me. I don't remember the specific year that I met Sam, but I think that it was in the early 1990s, during a Bassmaster Classic Outdoor Expo. Sometime after that, I started making a road trip annually from Missouri to Florida, with a primary objective being to fish with and learn from Sam on Lake Okeechobee. But I quickly discovered that laughing and sharing stories—fishing-related and otherwise—with this kind, gracious man and his wife drew me just as passionately.

I hope you enjoy this book about two American treasures, Sam Griffin and his mistress, Lake Okeechobee. And I hope that you profit from his home-spun wisdom, both about how to catch bass and life in general.

A special thanks to all those who helped make this book possible, but especially to Carol, Sam's wife of 60 years, who provided photos, information, and contacts.

Finally, articles contributed by others are acknowledged with their bylines. I wrote the rest.

Part I
Life on the Lake

1. In the Beginning

Sam Griffin didn't come into the world with a
fishing rod in his hand. But he picked one up at
an early age and rarely has put it down since.
Photo courtesy of Jake Griffin, his great nephew.

Samuel Asbury Griffin didn't come into this world with
a rod and reel in his hand. But if he had, he likely would
have known how to use it. Love of fish, fishing, and Lake
Okeechobee runs in his veins.

The son of commercial fisherman Joe Griffin, he was
born on Jan. 8, 1937, on the water, in a houseboat near
Clewiston. By the time that he was 7 or 8, he already was
assisting with the haul seine operation.

"Back then, the water was gin clear, with a layer of muck
on the bottom," Sam recalled. "There'd be mussel beds on

that and the bluegill spawned on top of those. I'd walk along those beds, playing, not working. But as I got older, I started having responsibilities."

One early job was to help keep the nets from snagging. As the Florida native described it, he used to "follow the cork line around, swimming, with no clothes on."

As young Sam was splashing about, his father really did work the lines, pulling the corks through pipes as the crew brought in the nets.

"I remember seeing fish jumping those cork lines," he said. "Big old bass would come across there."

To protect himself from flying fish, Joe Griffin "bought one of those Frank Buck cooter shell hats (pith helmet) and he would lay that hat on his shoulder where the fish hit him," Sam remembered.

"Sometimes, he would come in looking like he'd been in a barroom brawl, all skinned up. When he got older, he'd also put on a sweatshirt to cushion the blows.

"Just think, if someone dropped a 7- or 8-pound bass down on you from about 6 feet. That's gonna hurt!"

Of course, even if they didn't escape, bass weren't kept, since they weren't a commercial fish. But they certainly made harvest of catfish and panfish more exciting, and provided Sam with some of his first knowledge about his future love.

"When you get bass in a confined area and spook them, they're going to come out of the water," he said. "They can't go into the bottom. They have to come out."

Part I: Life on the Lake

One of his most vivid recollections of that occurred years later when he was fishing a grass bed. "An alligator on the bank came out and went under the grass," he said. "When that happened, a bass weighing about 6 pounds flew out of that grass, bounced on the back of my boat, and went back in the water."

Back in those early days, bass in most of the lake never saw a net, since commercials worked only about 20 percent of the lake, Sam said, "leaving the other 80 to produce fish."

"Some of the grandchildren of men working those waters in the 1940s are commercial fishermen today. "Only now they have to turn the crappie back," he added.

Indeed, commercial fishing is far more restricted today than it was 75 years ago on this lake long recognized as one of the nation's best sport fisheries for largemouth bass. Focus is on catfish, but harvest of bluegill and redear also is allowed.

After Joe Griffin and his crew netted crappie, bluegill, redear, and catfish, the catch was brought to a storage house that he built on the Industrial Canal in Clewiston, about 3/4 of a mile from where Sam was born. "We got started with that in '40 or '41, as men were starting to go off to war," Sam said.

Fish were dumped into vats of cold water and ice to prevent them from spoiling. Then, after they were chilled, they were packed with ice in boxes and shipped by railroad. Upon arrival in Jacksonville, they were re-iced and then sent on through the South and up the East Coast. Atlanta,

Birmingham, and the Carolinas were among the largest markets.

A Bass Fisherman Is Born

Perhaps not surprisingly, one of Sam's most vivid recollections of bass fishing as a child involved corporeal punishment administered by a hair brush.

A young man heading off to war pawned a Pflueger reel on a steel rod to Joe Griffin for some travelling money. And Sam took it from the there.

"One day I came home from school, and the diesel motors were running at the pumping station that pumped the water out of Clewiston," Sam said. "I knew that those old men in town would go down there at times like that because the fish would come up to feed and be in a frenzy in that swift water. They used Yellow Dude jigs, which were chicken feathers on lead-head jigs and they caught a lot of good fish."

So Sam "forgot" about his after-school chores, grabbed a rope stringer and the rod and reel and went fishing.

"I had me four or five fish on that stringer and I had this fish on when I heard a voice behind me," he recalled. "It was my mother's voice, and I knew I was in trouble so I grabbed my fish and started up the bank."

At the same time, he felt the first swat.

"About every 50 feet, I'd get that hair brush on the legs again, reminding me that I'd done wrong," he added.

Part I: Life on the Lake

Back at home, Sam's mother arranged for the fish to be cleaned and then told young Samuel to go to his bedroom and wait for this father.

"I knew that I was really going to get a whipping then," he said.

"That night, we had those fish for supper. It took me 10 years after that to figure out that I got a whippin' for getting supper. But my mother taught me a lesson. I no longer would go down there without seeking permission."

Well, his intentions were good anyway.

"After school, I was supposed to do my chores and then go fishing," Sam recounted. "But being a kid, I reversed that process. I got in trouble a number of times because I wanted to have fun and then do my work."

The young angler caught his first bass at a point created in a lake canal by a bridge on U.S. Highway 27.

"A few months later, I made three casts and caught six fish," he said. "They weighed about 2 pounds apiece, and I thought I was really a big shot. But then it was almost 20 years later before I caught another double. That's how it is in fishing."

The future luremaker's bait choices were limited in those early days.

"The lures I had were Creek Chub Darters in frog-spot silver flash," he explained. "One had a prop and one didn't. One was 3,000 series and one was 4,000 series."

He learned how to cast from the men he fished alongside at the canals.

"We all had the same kind of equipment," Sam said. "None of the reels had a drag. If you got a big fish on, the only way you could stop him was by thumbin' the line. If you didn't press down pretty hard, he'd burn the skin right off your thumb."

Eventually, young Sam started fishing out of a boat and his tactics changed. He used a Johnson weedless spoon with a pork rind trailer.

"If you pulled too fast, the spoon would turn over and over and kink your line," he recalled. "That taught me discipline.

Retrieved at just the right speed, though, the bait worked with action similar to today's buzzbait.

"The fish would come up and erupt on it," Sam said.

From trolling, he transitioned into learning where to cast the spoon, mostly to holes in vegetation such as needle grass (spike rush). He also educated himself about fishing bulrushes and massive beds of pepper grass, which might be as much a 1/3 mile wide and 3 miles along.

"Not every place held fish," he recalled. "Usually fish were where it was thicker, but thinner around the edges. The bass were in that thicker stuff. But when they were out roamin', I learned that I could catch them with topwaters instead of that spoon."

He also discovered that topwaters would take bass eating smaller fish that were feeding on the spawn of blue-gill beds in open water.

"We had no crankbaits. There was no such thing, until the River Runt came along," Sam said.

Sam also remembered using an early spinnerbait, the Shannon Twin Spin, and the Dalton Special, a topwater with a single prop on its tail.

"Today, I've mimicked that action with my Lil' Richard models," he said. "It still works.

"But the improvement that I've made is with the Mylar tail. After you jerk it and let it stop, that Mylar still is moving around and that attracts fish."

That subtle movement, he believes, draws bass that aren't on an aggressive bite.

"I figure it (Mylar) gives you about 25 percent more bites on a daily basis," Sam said.

"When they're smashing it, any kind of bait and action will catch 'em. We're all experts then. But when nothing is happening is what separates the men from the boys. You have to finesse 'em then."

Or you might have to work the bait faster or slower.

"My normal cadence is two jerks and let it sit," he explained. "But maybe you'll have to jerk it once and dibble it.

"To figure out what fish want, you have to watch them. If one comes up under your bait and rolls on it, it's not wanting to eat. But if you keep it there in front of him and make it enticing enough, he will eat it."

As he grew up and spent more and more time on Lake Okeechobee, young Sam learned that day fishing during a full moon can be one of the toughest times.

"All fish aren't feeding simultaneously at night," he said. "But many of them are. But what I've learned—and tour-

11

nament fishermen have provided proof of that—is that, no matter what the conditions, somewhere at any given time, the fish are biting. You just have to be smart enough to figure it out."

2. The Lake

Lake Okeechobee is about 6,000 years old. Based on geological surveys, that's an estimate from scientists who believe the lake was formed when the ocean receded, leaving a huge expanse of shallow water across the southern part of the state.

For most of that time, lake and sea remained connected and saltwater species frequently migrated into and out of the lake. Anglers caught redfish, snook, and flounder, along with largemouth bass and crappie. But construction of the Franklin Lock on the Caloosahatchee River more than 50 years ago destroyed that natural connection.

That's but one of many alterations made by man to Florida's largest lake during the 20th century. Sadly, nearly all of them have had negative, unintended consequences.

As an example, marsh fishing for bass is but a fraction of what it once was.

"People cut trails back into those marshes," Sam Griffin remembered.

"When the lake roamers (largemouth bass) started coming in November to spawn back there, they'd just keep on coming. They'd penetrate the grass, going way back in there. And traditionally, they'd go to the same places to spawn each year. Because of that, everybody took advantage of those trails to go catch them."

Big Sam and Big O

But that pattern began to decline in the late 1950s, as water demands on Okeechobee for agriculture and public water supply increased.

"Since 1958, we've had so many cycles of high and low water," he said. "Lots of areas that we fished back in the '40s, '50s, and '60s, we haven't fished in 15 or 20 years, because it's all grown up."

Compounding the problem has been the introduction of hydrilla, a fast-growing, exotic invasive plant, likely brought in unintentionally by boat trailers.

"We fish a lot of hydrilla, and it does hold fish," Sam added. "But hydrilla is like cattails. It's a mud builder. It grows in the summer and dies back in the winter, and all that stuff turns to mud. Bottom structure gets mud on it, and the fish won't bed there.

"Now, you have to go where the current flows through grass to clean it (mud) up and flush it out, where it dissipates along the shoreline," he said. "Then the wave action will put the mud back in the willow line, and that's where the muck starts building up. That's the cycle of the lake.

"Until they built the levee on the lake, it would flush out onto what's cow pasture now and cities and towns," Sam explained. " The lake probably was 1/3 and again bigger than what it is now before they crowded it up with the levee.

"Probably this day and age, they would have re-thought what they had done. They would have put the levee 3 or 4 miles way in and let the lake have its natural cycles of high and low water and flushing action. Back in those days, they wanted to reclaim the land, to farm and live. Those were just mistakes we humans make," he said.

"For instance after they channelized the Kissimmee River (which flows into the Big O), they realized that they made a big mistake. Of course they're rectifying that now to get filtering action again. And you had same thing around the lake."

That flushing action was just as important for the Everglades and Florida Bay to the south. Okeechobee overflow kept the 'glades vibrant and the saltwater bay fertile. But this massive and unique ecosystem came under assault and suffered permanent and long-term damage from the U.S. Army Corps of Engineers and state agencies, starting in the late 1920s. Of course, their intentions were the best: To provide for flood control and allow for development, both around the lake and in the Everglades.

These actions were prompted by the Great Miami Hurricane in 1926, which killed 300 people, and the Okeechobee Hurricane, which probably killed more than 2,000. In both cases, most of the deaths were caused by flooding, when strong winds drove water out of the lake and into surrounding communities.

That prompted the Florida Legislature to create the Okeechobee Flood Control District and it joined with the Corps, intending to prevent further disasters. The end result was construction of channels, gates, and nearly 140 miles of levees to prevent flooding. Additionally, it ended natural flushing action, turning the natural lake into a man-managed reservoir.

Big Sam and Big O

The Herbert Hoover Dyke system was expanded in the 1960s and now nearly encloses the lake, leaving Fisheating Creek as the only free-flowing tributary into the Big O.

According to the Florida Fish and Wildlife Conservation Commission, "Prior to the 1900s, water quality was characterized as clear and alkaline, and bottom sediments were described as 'clean sand.' Levee construction during the first half of the century confined the lake to a smaller area, eliminated overflow along the south shore, and facilitated back-pumping of excess water from the Everglades agricultural area into the lake.

"During the past 30 years, rising nutrient levels and periodic increases in the lake state regulatory schedules have decreased habitat quality and pushed the system near a hyper-eutrophic and ecologically undesirable state."

In 2010, during a public presentation in Glades County, *the Glades County Democrat* newspaper reported that Sam "mentioned that powerful federal and state agencies often keep the lake one foot too low to maintain its good health. During releases, the water level is pulled down too quickly, and the fishery is depleted of fresh water, even if it does not rain."

All of this is not to say that Lake Okeechobee still is not one of the nation's best fisheries—when it's right. But more and more during this century, it seems, it's not right. Of most concern have been massive algae blooms and, more recently, the die-off of beneficial aquatic grasses, likely caused by storms that stirred up the water, filling the lake with sediment, and preventing light penetration for months. Fortunately, as the sediment has settled and the water has cleared, grasses are returning.

Okeechobee Overload

Nearly 140 miles of levees added to prevent flooding have changed the Big O from a natural lake into a man-managed reservoir. Since then, the lake has suffered ecologically. But it remains one of the nation's best bass fisheries.

The following is an excerpt from an article that I wrote for B.A.S.S. Times in December 2016. It explains more about Big O water management, as well as how it damages coastal fisheries.

Big Sam and Big O

Debate rages about what to do with excess water from Lake Okeechobee. Laden with nutrients, it feeds algae blooms and kills fish when discharged by the Corps of Engineers into coastal waters on both sides of southern Florida.

But what about bass in the Big O? They're an integral part of a recreational fishery worth about $49 million to counties surrounding the 448,000-acre lake that is half the size of the state of Rhode Island.

"This is an iconic fishery, and yet all you hear about are the massive discharges and the algae blooms. You don't hear about the lake itself, other than it is the source," said Gene Gilliland, B.A.S.S. National Conservation Director.

Not to worry.

"They're doing great," said Andrea Dominguez, fisheries biologist for the Florida Fish and Wildlife Conservation Commission (FWC). "We're doing a survey now (early December) and are seeing a lot of fish over 16 inches, and a couple above 24.

"People are happy. They're catching fish, especially on the north end of the lake," she added. "Bass are healthy and growing."

But sadly for coastal fisheries and residents alike, the lake's eutrophic water must be channeled east and west when it rises too high, both to keep the aging dyke from being breached and prevent drowning of the marshes, which are key not just for the health of the fishery, but the entire Okeechobee ecosystem. Before the dyke was built and the Big O altered from a natural lake to a hybrid impoundment, high water flowed south. It replenished the

Part I: Life on the Lake

Everglades, which absorbed most of the nutrients, before sending the water on to vitalize Florida Bay.

The dyke was built to protect towns and farms south of the lake, following major hurricanes that struck South Florida during the 1920s, causing massive flooding and killing thousands. Additionally, the Corps installed water control structures to direct water via canals into the St. Lucie and Caloosahatchee estuaries.

With the lake walled off, much of the land around it was converted to agricultural use, with dairy farms and beef cattle ranching to the north and sugar cane and vegetable farming to the south. These added to the nutrient load of nitrogen and phosphorus already flowing into the Big O from the Kissimmee River watershed and developed areas to the north.

For decades runoff pollution has been a concern, both for the lake and the estuaries. But exceptionally high water, starting in January, forced heavier and more frequent discharges than normal, decimating the estuaries and garnering most of the headlines. In fact, an algae bloom covered 33 square miles in the southern portion of the lake during May, no doubt nourished by that same high water.

Algae blooms occur regularly in many of Florida's southern freshwater fisheries, but usually they appear later in the year, when the water is warmer. "They are very difficult to predict," said Terrie Bates of the South Florida Water Management District. "They move with the wind. They can form and dissipate in a week's time."

Fortunately, the Big O has proven resilient, thanks to its abundant aquatic vegetation, especially the fringe of bulrush on the lakeward side. It not only provides beneficial habitat directly, but helps dissipate wind and wave energy, allowing eel grass, spike rush, and pepper grass to grow in interior areas of the marsh.

Corps discharges of dangerously high water also helps, even as it damages coastal waters to the east and west.

"Excessive stages destroy this outer bulrush wall, which is then followed by damage to the interior marsh," said Amber Nabors, FWC's communications and marketing manager.

"FWC puts high priority on efforts to maintain a healthy diversity, abundance, and distribution of aquatic vegetation in the lake to support the abundant fish and wildlife resources there. We do this with both direct management actions and by closely working with partner agencies to influence water level management to include fish and wildlife benefits."

Those management actions include scraping, planting, and targeted herbicide treatments, as well as occasional burnings.

"We want the correct plants," said Dominguez. "We don't want stands of cattails to get too big, because we want the bulrush to grow."

Water hyacinths and water lettuce also are especially problematic because they grow so quickly and block waterways. The latter can be a problem both for navigation and for sustaining flow, which is critical for maintaining water quality.

High water and blocked flow are an especially lethal combination, as plants die and decompose, burning up dissolved oxygen in the water and releasing a "sewer gas" smell into the air. "It happens sometimes back in the marshes," said Sam Griffin, who grew up on the lake and guided for decades there. "When it does, the fish go around it to get back in the marshes to spawn."

Dominquez added, "We want to keep the waterways clear and we don't want just one plant (species). We want diversity, not monoculture."

Ideally, she explained, fall water levels will be high enough to allow bass to migrate back into the marsh. From winter into spring, they will recede, with stability during the summer, when fish can move out into the lake for refuge in cooler water if necessary.

Of course, storms and heavy rains in 2016 forced the Corps to intercede more than it does during a typical year. "Without those discharges, the vegetation would have been smothered," the biologist added.

Knowing the importance of Okeechobee's sport fishery and its ecosystem in general, FWC biologists talk weekly with the Corps, providing their opinions on what's best in terms of water levels, Dominguez explained. "We advocate if we see a need."

Nabors added, "FWC doesn't only manage for fish, but also waterfowl, wading birds, alligators, and other species."

Additionally, FWC has an intra-agency team working on Okeechobee/Everglades issues, as the ecological disasters on both coasts during 2016 forced both federal and state officials to accelerate the search for a solution to the lake's high water. Should flow be restored to the south? Should reservoirs be built north or south of the lake to store excess water? What can be done to lessen the nutrient load from agriculture and upstream development? The target phosphorus level for Okeechobee is 105 metric tons annually. In 2015, it was 450. About 37 percent of that came from land that drains into the Kissimmee River, according to the South Florida Water Management District. Sources include citrus groves, dairy farms, and neighborhoods as far north as the Orlando suburbs.

Whatever the solution, FWC intends to make certain that it will not negatively impact the Big O and its world-class bass fishery.

"All of the efforts in Everglades restoration, including reservoirs, water management north of the lake, discharges, and moving more water south, should ultimately allow flexibility and better management of the lake for ecological benefits, including sportfish management," said Nabors.

3. Uncle Joe's Fish Camp

Sam's father, Joe, started Uncle Joe's Fish Camp in the late 1940s, after Florida made commercial fishing illegal on Lake Okeechobee.

With the help of sons Sam and Richard, Joe Griffin continued to make a living by commercial fishing through World War II. But then in 1946, the state of Florida outlawed the harvest and sale of crappie and bluegill.

Big Sam and Big O

"Dad hired lawyers, like some others did, and fought the decision," Sam remembered. "But the masses wanted it shut down and that's what happened."

It stayed shut for more than a decade, before it re-opened with restrictions.

With the family in need of a new source of income, Sam said, his mother told his father, "If you can't beat the sport fishermen, then join them. And that's what he did.

"We got some Higgins red cedar boats and 5 horse-power Johnson outboards. They came in on a boxcar. The idea was that we'd rent those 10 boats on the Industrial Canal."

Meanwhile, a man from the commercial fishing crew had scavenged lumber and other debris from a hurricane, built himself a houseboat, and towed it to Liberty Point.

"We called him Uncle John and he was one of the few who did not drink," Sam recalled. "He was kind of a hermit who kept to himself.

"Uncle John said that people wanted to rent his boat, and we weren't renting many boats. So we let him have a couple of the boats.

"After awhile, he ended up with all 10 boats and then we added 10 more."

Eventually, the number climbed to 50 and Uncle Joe's Fish Camp was born. Back then, anglers sometimes had their own small outboards. But they were much more likely to rent boats than they are today.

"Mom negotiated the purchase of some state-owned land," Sam said. "My father logged cypress trees and built the cabins. Later, he built six duplex motel rooms and then a store and restaurant. "

Still more accommodations followed.

"We were 9 miles out of town," Sam remembered. "We put down a well. It was sulfur water and no one liked the smell."

Uncle Joe's Fish Camp attracted duck hunters as well as fishermen. In fact, one of the former named the camp.

"His dad brought him up there and he got to calling my dad 'Uncle Joe' and it stuck to him. Everyone started calling him Uncle Joe," Sam said.

"There was another Joe's Fish Camp and that had caused confusion, so the new name helped distinguish us."

In the beginning, fishermen and duck hunters stayed at the camp three or four days at a time. Then some of the anglers started staying a week during the winter.

"Eventually, they started coming down for the whole winter," Sam continued.

"Dad caught shiners and sold them for $2 a dozen, and people complained about the price. "Now, they're $20 to $25 a dozen."

Working on the Water

While young Sam mostly just enjoyed playing in the water when he accompanied his father to seine fish commercially, the new venture brought real work.

"I was growing all the time, learning more and more," he said. "I started guiding when I was 12. Back then, the compression on those motors was too much for me to crank 'em so the customer had to come back there and pull the rope.

"I could run it all right," Sam continued. "That lasted about a year and then I got strong enough to do it myself."

Along with the 5 horsepower outboard, the youngster's guiding tools included a push pole, oars, canoe paddle, and sculling paddle.

"The average depth (in Lake Okeechobee) is 6 feet and the water we were fishing in averaged 2 1/2 to 4 feet," he said. "I'd just push us along. If the wind was up, we'd drift fish."

When necessary, old-fashioned window weights were dropped to the bottom on ropes to slow the drift.

"The more I fished the marshes, the more I learned where the fish liked to stay," Sam said, explaining how, over time, he reduced his need for the oars and paddles.

Additionally, as they took customers fishing in the marshes, Sam and other guides dragged weighted saw blades behind their flat-bottom boats to cut trails that they could use again and again.

"Once the trails were cut, the outboard motors could take it from there," he recalled. "The problem was that, back then, we didn't have weedless propellers and the weeds would get around them really bad if we didn't cut trails."

Of course, despite the guiding, young Sam still found the time to fish.

"My brother Richard didn't like to fish nearly as much as I did," he said. "He didn't have the passion. That's something that I still have today.

Part I: Life on the Lake

"Today, I fish just as hard as I did when I was 7 years old," Sam laughed. "I just don't last as long.

"When I get out there, though, I forget about any problems or what the world is going through. It's just me and those green creatures in that water, with me trying to outfox 'em and knowing that I'm not going to most time. But still I like to try."

Whoops!

A couple of Sam's favorite stories about Uncle Joe's Fish Camp involved duck hunters. One of them, he added, "is about a shotgun not being compatible with a plywood boat."

"To build duck blinds in the marshes, hunters had to go into the really thick stuff," he explained. "Well, there are snakes in there."

And one of them dropped into the bow of a boat.

"In this case, the snake wasn't a cottonmouth," Sam said. "But to this hunter, every snake was a cottonmouth.

"He shot that snake and put a hole in the bottom of the boat. It was a good thing that it was in the bow. He and his partner got in the back of the boat so that the bow wouldn't be in the water, and that's how they came in."

Another time, a young man from Miami, hunting with his uncle, shot and killed a duck. Simultaneously, a Cub airplane dropped out of the sky nearby.

"He thought that he shot down the plane," Sam laughed. "But the guy was just having a fuel problem. He didn't actually crash. He came to an abrupt stop when his wheels hit the ground and it made a lot of noise.

"But it was that close to them that he really did think that he had done it. He pulled the trigger and the plane came down. They had to bring the pilot in.

"For a long time, the pilot told that story about the kid shooting him down."

Sam has a story to tell about himself too.

"I killed my first alligator illegally," he said. "It was 10 feet long and I was 14 years old.

"I was hunting with an experienced rogue, an outlaw. He never did anything that was legal. He wanted me to go with him. It was the only time I went."

Sam shot the beast with a shotgun. And then his criminal mentor followed with another blast into the gator's mouth after they wrangled him alongside the boat.

"We got it in the boat and across the seats," Sam remembered. "I was sitting on the back of the gator and he was sitting on the head. And about 15 or 20 minutes later, that gator started moving again.

"He shot him straight down into the head that time. We had to kill that gator twice."

4. A New Direction

Over time, Sam and Richard became more involved in running Uncle Joe's Fish Camp.

"He was inside, the pencil pusher, and I was outside with maintenance, taking care of things," Sam recalled. "Well, the winter business was good, but we decided that we wanted a better summer business.

"We decided that we'd build a swimming pool at Uncle Joe's Fish Camp."

At the time, the Griffins also owned Johnson's Fish Camp in Clewiston, which later became Roland Martin Marina.

"We had borrowed $50,000 to build that pool," Sam said. "Then Mr. Johnson wanted us to buy him out, but he wanted $100,000.

"Later, when he was strapped for cash, we gave him $50,000 and developed the place. So we had two fish camps: Uncle Joe's and Anglers Marina."

During the late 1970s, they sold Uncle Joe's and traded Anglers for a sugar cane farm.

"Although we didn't know it at the time, that was a big mistake," the luremaker said. "The sugar mill in Moore Haven went bankrupt and took us with it. We lost everything we had, except our homes.

"So…I was looking for something to do."

Coincidentally, Sam saw a lure business advertised in *Fishing Tackle Trade News*.

Sam started making and selling topwater baits around 1980. He still does so today, although on a smaller scale.

"I saw an ad for Ol' Ben's Baits in Shreveport, La.," he recalled. "My wife and I made a trip out there, and Ben Bacon treated us nicely. He had sidelined his hard bait business and was making rubber skirts and that's why he wanted to sell.

"So I bought it, hauled it back to Clewiston, and set it up."

The next step was for Sam to find a company that could provide bodies for the baits that he would paint and equip with hooks and other hardware. But Morgan Woodworks in Coweta, Okla., which supplied Bacon, didn't do that kind of work anymore.

Part I: Life on the Lake

"Lordy, I thought, I done bought a business here and can't get a wood body," Sam said. "I knew nothing about turning wood."

But he was willing to learn. Fortunately, too, the supplier had bait-turning equipment that it was willing to sell.

"I went to the banker, borrowed more money, and bought that," Sam said. "Then I had to get wood."

To get a reasonable price, though, he had to buy a boxcar load.

"The building that I had in Clewiston was too small, so I found one in Moore Haven that had a building and a big lean-to shed for about $10,000 worth of lumber.

"Then I started making my own bodies. I was making a finished lure from a piece of wood, packaging it, and trying to sell it to distributors," Sam said. "I was in competition with people who had been in the lure business for many years.

"We had five people working for us, but we struggled. We also sold bodies to other small companies to help keep things going."

His original offerings included Ol' Line Sides, a variation of the Heddon Zaragossa walking bait, and Hobo, developed from a body that Sam was turning for another company. His 1980 business card read, "Griffin Lures Mfg. of Sam's Baits."

Over time, he also developed Sam's Woody, Sammy Shad, Sam's Chub, Pop'n Sam, Sugarwood Spoon, and Salty Pop.

Big Sam and Big O

In 1983, the budding innovator used foil on his baits for the first time. He later created the hatchback paint pattern, as he developed a reputation for topwater baits noted for their impressive finishing.

Sam also recognized that water penetration was a problem for wood baits, because it caused them to expand just enough to crack their paint and/or protective coats. He designed bodies specifically to avoid that problem.

By 1989, Sam's lure-making skills had attracted the attention of one of the largest lure companies in the country at the time, Luhr Jensen & Sons of Hood River, Ore.

"Phil Jensen called and wanted to talk to me," Sam said. "I ending up selling the business to him.

"Just rednecks from the country, we'd never been to Oregon, so Carol (his wife) and I flew out there. We spent one night in a motel on the Pacific Ocean and then drove to Hood River, where we closed the deal."

Some of Sam's creations for the company included Jerk'n Sam, Nippin' Sam, Lil' Chris, Bass Baffler, and Wobble Pop. He also redesigned other Jensen lures, making them better balanced.

"We had the ability to turn every bait that Jensen had, including the Dalton Special and Nip-I-Diddee," Sam explained. "We turned the bodies, drilled them, and painted them, but we didn't put the hooks or hardware on them.

"We then shipped them in bulk to Hood River, and they'd hook them, package them, and distribute them. We were making 12,500 topwater baits a week with 22 employees, all of them women. That went on for a few years."

Then Jensen decided to move its lure-making business to Mexico, and asked Sam to supervise production.

"We had all kinds of problems getting equipment in there," he remembered. "Also, I was down there and Carol was back in Florida. It was supposed to last six months and I was there at least two years.

I wasn't liking that at all."

Then came another pivotal point in Sam's career as a luremaker: He had to drive a van more than 400 miles from the plant in Ensenada, Mexico, to Las Vegas, for ICAST, the fishing industry's annual tackle show.

"The crowning blow that made me quit and come home was when the transmission went out in the middle of the desert and the temperature was 110 degrees," he said. "I was stuck on the side of the road for two hours, with no cell phone back then and waiting for a state trooper to come by.

"But none did."

With no other choice, Sam decided to see if the engine would start. Fortunately, it did.

"I went up this hill slowly," he remembered. "When I got to the top, I went down in the emergency lane and finally I was in flat country. From there, he nursed the vehicle into Las Vegas.

"Carol flew out and went back with me to Ensenada," Sam continued. "We stayed two nights, and then I told her that I was quitting and going home."

The two drove cross country and down the Florida peninsula to Sam's beloved Lake Okeechobee.

"I didn't know what I was going to do," he said. "But I immediately went back into the lure business since I didn't have a no-compete clause. I knew how to turn them by hand, a single bait at a time on a lathe."

He also resumed guiding through his Legends Guide Service.

The Lil' Richard, a twitch bait, and the Offset Sam, a slush bait, probably are the two most well known offerings under the Custom Lures by Sam label. He also made a line of baits called "The Naturals," which featured coatings of western diamondback rattlesnake skin, covered in clear plastic finish.

For years, Sam maintained a small facility and retail store in Moore Haven, content not to compete with the big boys, before downsizing to his garage. And, at 83, he's still making lures and going fishing.

After getting to know Sam, Phil Jensen called him "a legend in our time" because of his lure-making skills and innovations.

5. Sam and Carol

Carol Daughtrey's first date with Sam Griffin came when she was just a few weeks shy of 16. He was an older man, already graduated from Clewiston High School and working as a guide at his father's fish camp. They attended a high school football game in Belle Glade, along with her father.

"Clewiston is a small town and there weren't many places to go on dates," Carol remembered. "Just football games in the fall and to the movies once a week."

Well…there was someplace else. At least for Sam Griffin there was. Lake Okeechobee.

"I have always said that Sam made sure I loved to fish before we married," she said. "He not only taught me to fish with a rod and reel; he also taught me to drive. I was so young! Sam and I were married on June 7, 1959, just nine days after I graduated from high school."

As luck would have it, Carol's father also like to fish and often accompanied them there as well.

"I remember one time we got caught in a bad thunderstorm while we were out on the lake," Carol recalled. " Lightning was popping all around us so Sam had us get overboard so our heads were lower than the top of the boat. I still am not sure that was a safe thing to do, but we survived to go fishing another day.

"We would get overboard and fish while wading too," she added. "We put the fish we caught on stringers and tied them to our belts.

"But one day I turned to look behind me and was surprised to see an alligator swimming towards me. Needless to say, I got myself back into the boat and never waded again."

Long before they started going on fishing "dates" and even before they attended that football game with Carol's father, the two had become acquainted.

"It seems like I have always known Sam," she said. "Clewiston is a small town and was even smaller back in the '50s. I grew up next door to the Swindle family. There were five Swindle boys and Sam was a best friend to Eddie.

"My mother worked at a restaurant in a truck stop located just west of Clewiston," Carol added. "When I was 15, I would go help her on Friday and Saturday nights and during the summer. Sam would stop in on his way home from Hank's Pool Room to have a burger and coffee. He began to stop in more frequently and finally got the nerve to ask me out."

Sam escorted Carol to both her junior and senior proms—after he had taken her older sister, Edith, previously. As a result, brother Richard dubbed Sam "the prom king."

Their June honeymoon consisted of a visit to the beach at Naples and then up to Lake Kissimmee for some bass fishing.

"I have to admit that I was a little disappointed because our car had not been decorated as newlyweds' cars often were," Carol said.

Part I: Life on the Lake

The following morning, however, they discovered that Sam's brother had put a little surprise inside the car—a package of raw fish.

"This was summer in Florida and the fish were really beginning to smell," she added.

"Sam endured the beach for a couple of days and then we headed to Lake Kissimmee."

Enroute, they stopped for gas in Arcadia and discovered another of Richard's surprises, when they saw flies swarming around one of the hubcaps.

"Yep! Richard had put more fish in the hubcap and, boy, were they smelly," Carol said. "I have a picture of Sam cleaning the hubcap."

(Richard died of cancer in 1979. In his memory, Sam named one of his most popular topwater baits "Lil' Richard.")

Shortly after Carol and Sam were married, Sam joined the National Guard.

"He felt that would be better than being drafted because he would not be away from his family or his family's business as long," she remembered. "He just had to do six months of training and then a meeting one weekend a month and two weeks away in the summer for more training.

"Well, it didn't quite work out that way because his unit was called to active duty during the Berlin Crisis in 1961 and he spent a year at Fort Lee, Virginia. I was able to go with him. Our son was not yet a year old. It was an adventure as I had never been out of Florida and I had never seen snow. The snow was beautiful, but it did not take long for this Florida girl to have her fill. Fortunately, we did not go to war and were back home the next year."

A few detours notwithstanding, fishing always has been a part of the couple's life together.

"First there were the fish camps and then his lure-making business and fishing tournaments," she explained. "We fished a couples tournament trail together and had a lot of fun.

"I even fished a few Bass'n Gal tournaments, but soon realized that those ladies were serious! Sam had spoiled me over the years by doing almost everything for me. Now I was expected to do it myself. Needless to say, I didn't last long.

"Sam enjoyed fishing tournaments and was able to fish some of the big ones," Carol said. " I worked but was able to plan my vacations around some of those tournaments.

"The fishing industry has afforded us opportunities to travel to places that we probably would not have gone. We have met many interesting people over the years and remain friends with a number of them."

Sam and Carol have two children, Samuel Joseph born on Jan. 5, 1961, and Karen Christine born on May 30, 1964, as well as five grandchildren.

"While both of our children are good at fishing, neither really has the interest," Carol said. " They both live busy lives, but try to go with their dad several times a year because they know he loves to take them."

Sam and wife Carol with their granddaughter, Katelyn Fabian.

Later in life, they were blessed with Cougie, a 21-year-old, who's still living at home. Mostly, she just likes to eat fish.

"We call Cougie our 'grand cat' because she belonged to our son who was married previously to Shelia and they had two cats," Carol said.

Following a series of misfortunes and Sheila's death from cancer, Cougie joined Sam and Carol.

Nightly they hold her with a towel and put drops in her ears to protect them from mites. Sam and Cougie often engage in conversations about the day's events. If a visitor is sitting in Cougie's place, she will tell him, and she will join overnight guests in their bedrooms if the doors are not closed.

"She has brought joy to our lives," Carol said.

Attending the Saint Martin's Episcopal Church in Clewiston has as well.

"We began going there together during a particularly bad time in our marriage," Carol said. " Through much counseling, many prayers and by the grace of God we overcame the difficulties. Without God in our lives, there would be no Sam and Carol."

Part II
Bass and Baits

6. Sam Shares Strategies

Sam Griffin guided bass fishermen on Lake Okeechobee for more than a half century, as well as fished tournaments. He also spent decades creating and field-testing baits that will catch bass anywhere, from Canada to Mexico. Combine the two skill sets and he arguably he *is* the authoritative source for topwater fishing generally and bass fishing on Lake Okeechobee specifically.

Added to that, he's a great teacher. Every angler I've spoken to, who's fished with Sam, has told me that. But mostly I speak from personal experience. I don't even remember how long that I've been learning, but probably since the mid 1990s.

What I've discovered is that Sam not only is knowledgeable, but he loves to share what he knows. He's also patient; I've never seen him angry. And he's unflappable, whether a storm is approaching, a swarm of bees sounds ominously close, or an agitated alligator follows a bait all the way back to the boat.

Following are some of the topwater tips that I've learned from Sam over the years. Along with his baits, most of these strategies will work anywhere.

"My big things are to be confident and have patience,"
Sam said.

"I'll fish behind people throwing worms and crankbaits and catch fish they bypass. I like to fish that topwater slower and let 'em read the menu.

"Most of the time, people fish a topwater too fast," the lure designer added. "They're just pulling and pulling. I'd say that 85 percent of the time, the bite comes when the bait is still or coming to a stop."

With poppers, chuggers, and prop baits, Sam usually will jerk the bait twice, creating slack in the line and allowing the bait to sit. Then he will swing the rod tip toward the bait, taking in line, and repeat the sequence. With a popper, he might jerk just once.

"Pay attention and fish will let you know what they want," he said. "If you are fishing too fast, they will follow but not hit."

"Early and late is a myth," said Sam.

"Those are not the only times to throw a topwater. People used to fish two or three hours before work and then come home and fish two or three hours. That's the way that got started. It wasn't that the fish quit biting. It was that they quit fishing. After work, they'd go out and fish some more and maybe catch some more fish.

"I catch a lot of fish in the middle of the day, and I've found that 10 to 2 is the most productive time for big fish (on Lake Okeechobee)."

Part II: Bass and Baits

Topwaters aren't just for warm water.

"You can catch bass consistently on top in water that is 50 degrees or above," the longtime guide said. "Usually in colder water, you want to fish extremely fast or extremely slow, not in between."

The popper is a good choice for colder water, he added, because you can keep it in one place longer and because its tail sits down in the water, making it easier for the bass to take.

That same quality means the popper also is a preferred topwater when fish are holding tight to cover.

"I tell people that when the water temperature gets below 45 degrees (on Lake Okeechobee) to pick up a worm and get down there (deeper water) or go do something else like play golf or go to Disney World."

The same topwater bait will work anywhere.

"It's a matter of confidence," said Sam. "That's why there are regional favorites."

Not every topwater bite is explosive.

"A bass can suck the bait in like a vacuum cleaner or hit it so hard that it knocks off the paint," Sam revealed.

In general, louder and larger baits will draw more aggressive bites. Smaller, more subtle baits will get the "suckers."

"In cold weather and in calm water, when you're using a small bait, it's really important to watch your line, just like you would with other baits," Sam said. "That's because you're more likely to get a sucking bite.

"With a soft, suck bite on the back of the bait, don't set the hook hard," he cautioned. "Instead, lift up and reel. Otherwise you'll pull the hook out. When you do get a fish this way, it's usually hooked on the edge of the mouth or even the outside."

Topwaters aren't just for calm water.

"Take what the weather gives you," said Sam. "In rough weather, you can throw in the 'wind rows' in grass. And you can throw in troughs between waves. Most of the time, you'll want a faster retrieve in rough water, to take the slack out of your line."

With topwaters, most fish are caught on the front hook.

That means it is important to have a bigger, stronger hook there.

Dress up the back hook.

Sam has learned that he gets 25 percent more bites when he puts pearlescent Mylar tinsel on the back hooks.

The Mylar will continue to subtly move after the bait stops, and, if the sun is shining, Sam explained, "it will pick that up and broadcast that.

"If you can tell that you've got a fish looking at it, just twitch it, but not hard. Just keep moving it a little," he added.

Part II: Bass and Baits

"That fish might not be hungry but it (the bait) is there, in its environment and that fish is thinking, "What am I gonna do with that?"

Sam likened the situation to what he calls the "drumstick theory." A man has just eaten his fill at Sunday dinner. But he spies a leftover drumstick on a platter as he walks through the kitchen. He's not really hungry, but . . .

Sam stumbled upon the benefits of Mylar by accident. He used white bucktail on back trebles for years, but finally decided that it was too expensive. He went to Mylar to help hold down costs and, because it comes in a band, it doesn't have to be tied.

On the negative side, Mylar doesn't hold up well to needle-nose pliers, often used by anglers to remove hooks from fish.

"What are fish thinking? I don't know," Sam said. "They're not talking. But by doing little things, especially with that Mylar, you just might get him to hit. A lot of times it works. Other times, nothing works."

If more than one bass is around, he added, "then you've got a competition mentality." That means it's easier to provoke a bite.

Of course, the easiest time to catch bass on top is when they're feeding and in what Sam calls "a frenzy mode. That's when they have a top predator mentality," he explained. "You don't even have to move the bait then."

7. Tony Meets Lil' Richard

By Tony Manganello

Tony Manganello fished tournaments with his topwater mentor.

While attending a charity fundraiser in 2006, I decided to check out the silent auction items displayed on a table. I noticed an item for a guided fishing trip on Lake Okeechobee, a place my brother Bobby had always dreamed about fishing. The bidding went back and forth between another fellow and me, but I had to have it and eventually won.

Excited by my winning, I immediately called my brother and told him that he needed to plan a trip to Florida. Once he agreed, I put the plan in place and booked our trip with Sam Griffin and the date was set. I booked a room for us at Roland Martin Marina and Resort and even had custom logoed fishing shirts made with "Big Ass Bass Brothers 2007 World Tour" wrapped around a bass breaching the water embroidered on one side and our names on the other.

I wanted this to be the trip of a lifetime for us. But I had no idea just how amazing and life-changing this trip would turn out to be.

In May 2007, we checked in at Roland's and unpacked our stuff, drank a cold beer, and set up our rods for the following morning. Early the following morning, I'm not sure about my brother, but, for me, it felt like I had only a short nap. I tossed and turned all night, just thinking about the day ahead. We gathered our belongings, grabbed a biscuit and coffee, and headed out to meet Sam at the pre-arranged location.

He greeted us with this huge smile on his face, as if he were more excited about the trip then we were. He firmly gripped my hand as if we were old friends. Bobby and I loaded our gear on the boat and we jumped into Sam's truck for a short ride to the ramp. I remember Sam laughing and saying, "It looks like you guys have everything you need."

As he drove, Sam told us about the severe drought and water levels being the lowest they had been in years. He did, however, reassure us by sharing his knowledge of the lake. In fact, he was the guy who marked the channels for other boaters to navigate safely.

Part II: Bass and Baits

As we motored out of Moore Haven Canal and into Moonshine Bay, Sam pointed out landmarks. "This is the community hole," he said. "Those are navigation poles marking the channel. That way is Fisheating Creek."

He seemed genuinely excited to share his knowledge and he certainly had our interest.

When we reached our destination, the Monkey Box, Sam asked if we had ever heard the most famous fish call. Then the big man stood up, put his hands around his mouth and yelled, "Here fishy, fishy!"

We burst out laughing, but almost immediately we started catching bass, Bobby with a jig and me with a crank-bait.

We were having a ball, bringing in one fish after the other, and they kept getting bigger. Finally, I decided that I wanted to switch baits and Sam said, "That makes sense. Your lure is working great, but you should probably try something different."

So, he handed me a lure and said, "Tie this on. It's called a Lil' Richard."

This gesture had nothing to do with self-promotion, but we quickly learned that Sam was in the lure-making business and this was one of his creations. He gave me a 30-second lesson on how to work it. Soon enough, I had a big girl crash on it and I was hooked!

Not to be outdone by my catch, Sam stood up again, placed his hands around his mouth, and hollered, "Fishy, fishy in the brook, please come and bite my hook!"

We couldn't stop laughing!

Big Sam and Big O

This guide trip was supposed to be for 6 hours, but we fished for 10. Sam was wonderful. He told Bobby and me that he was enjoying it. He said that normally his time was spent untangling lines. But with us, he was able to just enjoy the time on the water. We caught 20 fish over 5 pounds, with the biggest being 8-plus. It was a trip of a lifetime and my brother's grin was ear to ear. To this day, 13 years later, my brother and I still talk about that trip.

For many, that's where the story would end after hiring Sam Griffin as a guide. But for me. it was just the beginning. It ignited a passion for bass fishing and a love for Lake Okeechobee. I've always enjoyed fishing, but I now wanted to learn more and become a better fisherman. I called Sam to purchase a few more of those magic baits, the Lil' Richard. We talked about me wanting to join a fishing club and my desire to become a better fisherman. We probably spent a half hour or more talking about that and also talking about the trip with my brother.

A couple months later, when I called to place another order, his first question was, "How's your brother?"

I started fishing with a local club and did well; for Sam that is. I became the largest local, non-commission salesperson for Sam's lures, especially the Lil' Richard. We talked more frequently, as I needed to place more orders. And "How's your brother?" became "How's your family?"

In one of the conversations, I mentioned that I had a tournament coming up on Lake Okeechobee and I was a bit nervous. Sam offered to take me out fishing to help me get comfortable.

Part II: Bass and Baits

Our friendship blossomed and Sam and I fished more and more together. He became my fishing partner for the Gambler Lures open tournaments.

My fishing skills got better, but I wasn't known on Lake Okeechobee for my fishing, I was known for my sandwiches. Every tournament Sam and I fished, I was in charge of the food, which always included a package of chocolate chip cookies, since Sam has a bit of a sweet tooth. My buddy Jay's wife used to bake pecan pies that we would deliver to Sam and Carol. We would sit for hours, eating pie and listening to Sam's fish stories.

As my passion for bass fishing continued to grow, I started fishing BFL events and Sam was always just a call away for advice. At some point, though, my passion changed, from wanting to fish to teaching kids how to fish. Sam was a big inspiration for me to start Reel Fishing Charities. He spent much of his time teaching people how to fish and creating memories that would last a lifetime. At all of my kids events, you can find me paying tribute to my buddy Sam by putting my hands around my mouth and belting out, "Here fish, fishy!"

Thank you, Sam. My greatest day of fishing was spent with you, my brother. My best tournament was with you as my partner, weighing in 33.5 pounds of bass on that cold, rainy day.

Sam Griffin, my friend, you created those memories for me just like you did for many others. And when I do get to go fishing, I have a Lil' Richard tied on and I think of you and smile.

8. The Starting Lineup

"Your first fish on topwater is like your first kiss. You never forget it," is one of Sam Griffin's most popular and often repeated sayings.

That's probably because so many people can identify with it. I know I can.

My first topwater bass exploded on a yellow Hula Popper, and, decades later, I can relive that moment as vividly in my mind, feeling nearly the same excitement, as when it occurred on a cool, fall afternoon at a farm pond. It is one of my favorite memories, and that popper is one of my most prized possessions.

In the decades since, I've caught thousands of bass larger than the one that I caught that fall day, including more than a dozen that weighed 10 pounds or more. And I have caught some of those lunkers on Sam's wooden surface baits, mostly the Offset Sam. (More on that later.)

But the ones that gave me the most enjoyment were not necessarily the heaviest. They were the ones that came on top.

You see, that first bass on top—the one that I'll never forget—set my course for life in terms of bass fishing. From that moment on, I remembered how much that blowup excited me, and I wanted more. I needed more. I was an addict.

And that's why I'm so blessed to have Sam as a friend. It's as if some higher power led the student to his teacher.

Additionally, throwing Sam's lures are my preferred way to feed my addiction.

As you read about these baits, keep in mind that they're not just for Lake Okeechobee, even though that's where Sam created them and that's where they're the most popular and most recognized. Bass will hit them anywhere they will take a topwater. Sam reports that one of his creations yielded a 12-pounder in Georgia and another an 11 "up around Orlando."

"They catch smallmouths in the 6-pound range," he added. "Up on the St. Lawrence Seaway, smallmouths love the Lil' Richard."

Lil' Richard

The Lil' Richard, a swish or twitch bait, is the one that I use the most often, probably because it is the most versatile. I've caught bass with it from Canada to Mexico, including smallmouth and spotted bass, as well as largemouths. On the Ozark streams near my home, I now throw it instead of the Tiny Torpedo, another of my favorite topwaters from childhood.

Sam named this bait in honor of his older brother, who died of cancer in 1979. It is one of at least 10 baits that he created and produced, starting in 1993, when he returned to Lake Okeechobee and started Custom Lures by Sam. Over the years, he estimates that it has been his No. 1 seller and fish catcher.

"It has similar action to the Dalton Special, which is what I wanted to mimic because it does so well," Sam said, adding that it lies flat on the water.

Additionally, it's variation of the Jerkin' Sam that the Florida native made for Luhr Jensen, only it has a ski nose instead of a "V" mouth.

Sam and friend Dave Burkhardt with a bass caught by the latter on the Lil' Richard.

"I will jump that bait sometimes, from hole to hole, especially if I'm fishing lily pads," he explained.

"You're gonna get hung up sometimes, but not as much as what you'd think, if you pay attention to what you're doing. You do have to have some open water. I like to fish it around edges and in flats."

The Lil' Richard was one of his favorites for clients to use when he was guiding because it often allowed them to catch "forgiving fish." In other words, bass were actively feeding out away from the vegetation and accuracy wasn't necessary to get their attention and provoke bites.

"Fish like that forgive individuals for not being so good," he laughed. "With good fishermen, you can fish closer to the banks of grass and smartweed and peppergrass edges. That's not just with the Lil' Richard, but all the (topwater) baits."

In general, here's how to fish the Lil' Richard, in Sam's own words:

"After the impact rings move away, with your rod down, jerk the lure hard two times, 'dead stick' it, and then repeat.

"The Lil' Richard will cut through thin grass and stay clean.

"Fish the thin areas or open pockets in the thick grass using short twitches, hopping it over the heavier cover. In open water, use the Lil' Richard the same as the Moonshine Special. When in schooling fish, use short, but fast jerks with a pause, then repeat."

Whether you're throwing the Lil' Richard or any other topwater bait, always pay attention to what the fish are doing, especially if they're not biting, Sam emphasized.

"If there's an explosion at the boat, the fish are telling you to slow down," he said. "In that case, you're got to give the fish time to read the menu.

"Fish have their own pace. They're either going to react or think it through. And when they start thinking, that's when they can get hard to catch. You have to finesse them. You have to slow down the cadence."

Offset Sam

Author with one of the many bass that he's caught with the Offset Sam, his favorite lure for big fish.

Big Sam and Big O

The Offset Sam might be the least well known of Sam's lineup, but it's my favorite for prompting explosive strikes, often from big bass.

I've watched guides stand open-mouthed and speechless after seeing an attack on an Offset Sam for the first time.

In fact, I've reached the point with this bait where I fish mostly for the strikes instead of hooking and landing the bass. I'm addicted to the excitement. Time after time, I've seen bass jump totally out of the water to land on this bait with a stunning "kersplash!" Other times, they attack from below and charge high into the air with the bait in their mouths.

One extraordinary morning on Mexico's Lake El Salto, I had two such explosive misses consecutively in the same spot. My heart racing and my hands shaking, I decided to try it once more and this time I hooked the fish that wouldn't quit. It weighed 12 pounds.

Offset Sam is a "slush" bait. With props at the head and tail, it throws up lots of spray as it cuts loudly across the surface. Bass typically hit when it is paused.

"Offset" refers to the fact that the middle set of trebles is placed to the side of the belly. Sam believes that this placement enhances hookups, and I believe him.

I like the white/black back and white/green back.

Here's what Sam has to say about the bait that bears his name:

"The offset of the belly hook is the heart of it. The concept comes from years ago, when we had those meat-fish catching baits with five treble hooks.

"Those baits would hold a fish, all right, but they'd also tear him up pretty good.

"I believe in catch and release. But when you release the fish, you want to put him back in good shape.

"The belly hook is 30 degrees from the center of the bait, but it still allows it to sit flat on the water. Then, like Chinese handcuffs, the hooks are pulling against each other (when the fish is hooked).

"You get better hookups and the fish stay hooked better, but you don't have the five-hook concept that tears up the meat. You have efficiency without all the hooks."

Moonshine Special

Named for Okeechobee's Moonshine Bay, this bait is similar in action to the Offset Sam, only with smaller diameter and slimmer profile. Sam said that he modeled it after the Devil's Horse.

Additionally, the bait can be zoomed around cover like a buzz bait, Sam said. "Working the lure fast in an area where fish are holding and then working it slowly through the same area, can produce very hard strikes."

What makes this wooden lure different from others of similar design is screw-eye hook construction instead of hook hangers.

"This allows hooks to swing freely under the bait instead of gouging into wood. That extends the life of the bait," Sam said.

"I put a bead on front of bait," he added. " I use a screw eye, hollow bead, propeller, and a then a cup washer. This leaves a space in there. "You don't want the prop totally vertical. You want it so it will lie flat at about a 30-degree angle. It picks up water better and makes a better swoosh. The bead help prevent the line from overriding and getting on the prop."

And here's a secret from Sam that you've probably never thought about: Do *not* move the lure as you reel in slack line.

"While the lure is stopped, the fish may be thinking about it," he said. "Swimming the lure a little as you retrieve the slack will break his attention."

Pop'n Joe

Sam named this popper for his son, Samuel Joseph.

As with most of this type baits, it sits down in back.

"The concave nose picks up water and that makes the pop." Sam said.

"I like to use it when it gets real cold (water temperature of 50 degrees or below)."

He also has a Creek Popper, which doesn't make quite as much noise.

With popper, he explained, "you're trying to bring fish up off the bottom. But you'll want to twitch them (the baits) as much as pop them."

What makes poppers effective in cold water, when fish aren't moving much, is that you can work them for a longer time in a small area.

"They'll sort of dip over and that reduces the forward motion," Sam said. "The popper will go maybe 4 inches when you pop it, and then the water will push it back.

"That's why it's good in holes in hydrilla and lily pads too. From 11 to 2, if the sun is out and you see black holes in the hydrilla, pitch to them with a popper."

As a moving bait, meanwhile, its action resembles the Jitterbug, Sam said. "It erratically moves water and you can get strikes doing that."

Florida Shad

According to Sam, the Florida Shad's action also is similar to that of the Offset Sam. It has two props, but a smaller body and just two treble hooks instead of three. On a retrieve, the props rotate in the same direction, which turns the bait about 30 degrees in water. Glittery sides help attract attention.

Fish Creek Darter

Sam calls the Fish Creek Darter "a knockoff of Creek Chub Darter, with the same action."

"It's an erratic topwater bait," he added. " When you let it sit, it tends to change ends. Then, when you pull it the next time, it goes the other direction.

"There's a certain amount of burble to it, like a popper," Sam said. "And it can be a semi-surface crankbait. You have to sweep your rod to get it to bite, to get the lips down into water. The pull point on top of the head helps it swing and sway like a crankbait."

Because this is a bait for aggressive fish, the former guide explained, he doesn't use Mylar on the tail. "That would drag the back of the bait and take away the action."

Other Baits

Sam's additional offerings have included the Lil' Zip, Creek Walker, Zip'n Sam, Lil' Katie, STP, and Magnum Peacock.

The Lil' Zip is a prolific bass producer, Sam believes, because of its smaller size, with action similar to many of his other baits. "I've seen bass go right up on a sandbar chasing it," he said.

"The dressed tail with its oversized prop causes the zipping noise," he added. "Faster action causes the lure to 'walk the dog' in a modified way."

The Lil' Katie is Sam's signature crankbait. Named for his granddaughter, it's a shallow runner. (He also is working on a walking bait, Mighty Matt, in honor of his grandson.)

The STP is a double prop, three treble, designed for snook, tarpon, and peacock bass, while the peacock baits are magnum versions of the Moonshine Special and Lil' Richard.

Sam also crafted collector's versions of some of his baits, wrapping them in the skin of western diamondback rattlesnakes.

9. What Makes a Good Topwater Bait

A customer once asked Sam to make some Lil' Zips for him in clear.

"I told him that if he could find me a clear tree, I'd make them," Sam recalled with a chuckle.

Of course, that's because his wooden topwaters are made with—what else?—wood.

"I used to use all sugar pine," he luremaker said. "Now, I'm using red and white cedar, handpicked. I'll go through about 30 pieces of lumber to find two boards that I can use.

"Those will have fewer knots in them. That's the key. Lots of sap springs out from those knots, making the wood too hard and too heavy so it doesn't float right.

"I cut the wood off in rectangular blocks and each bait is turned individually."

Sam added that wood is better than plastic because of its bulk and weight.

"Plastic reacts too quickly because it's hollow inside," he said.

"You want a bait that sits a little down in the tail, and sometimes even more.

"The farther that it sits down, the less it moves forward. Also, you can put weight on the tail hook to slow forward movement even more."

Of course, as Sam is quick to explain, reducing movement allows you to keep a topwater active in one place longer, which can be especially effective in cold water and/ or when fish are "reading the menu," instead of feeding aggressively.

Color

"The fish is looking at the belly of the bait so that's the color that is important," Sam said. "It's not looking at the top. A nice, pretty color on top is to catch fishermen. It doesn't have much to do with catching fish."

Sam acknowledged that just about every angler has his or her preference, and his is black and white. "It's what I grew up with and what I have confidence in.

"I probably throw that 75 percent of the time," he added. "On occasion, I'll go off the wall and use a yellow bait, with some black on it. When a bait with a single prop torques over as you pull it, the fish can see that black."

Of the 26 colors that Sam uses, green, white, and baby bass are popular options, he added, while some want pure black. "They probably would use it even without eyeballs," he laughed.

"But baits have to have eyeballs or most people won't buy them. It's a between-the-ears thing. Not the fish's either. The fisherman's. It's not a problem for me, though. It's funny."

Fishermen also like silver and gold foil, as well as white and orange bellies and black backs. "Those depict shiner and shad colors," Sam said.

"In tea-colored water (tannic stain) baits with orange bellies produce more fish than those with white bellies," he continued, adding that white bellies are better in clear water."

Sam recalled making some baits for someone who specified that he wanted no red under the nose or on the tail. But the employee doing the painting forgot and red was applied. Sam made it right, taking those baits back and delivering others with no red to the customer.

"About a week later, I was out fishing and throwing one of those baits that I took back," Sam remembered. "That guy was out there too. I was tearing up the fish, and he wasn't doing so well. When he asked what I was using, I showed him that bait with the red on it. You just never know."

Sides

Most of a bait's design is on its sides, Sam said.

"The bottom should be a solid color with an orange or red splash on the throat. The back should be a darker color.

"But the sides can have some glitter. Then, when the bait torques over, they pick up the sun. That translates into strikes coming from a farther distance. The Mylar does the same thing.

"In general, bait designs are more for the fishermen than the fish. I make baits with all solid colors that would catch fish. But I'd never sell a one."

Action

In short, action is more important than color, Sam believes.

"Usually it's the action," he qualified.

"If you twitch it at the wrong time, a fish might not hit it," he said. "On the other hand, if you don't twitch it at the wrong time, he might hit it. You have no way of knowing. And if you could figure that out, you could catch fish all the time."

A little red on the neck or tail can help, he added. "I don't think that fish scrutinize a reactionary bait. But if they're taking their time looking at a bait, they'll see certain things."

Bait Size

Sam is a firm believer in the old angler adage "match the hatch."

"Fish key on the size of the bait that they're feeding on," he said. "Sometimes it's hard to catch schoolers because of that.

"Sometimes if you're not catching fish and they're feeding, throw a smaller profile topwater bait and don't move it. Just let it sit there.

"You will find one that will hit it in a minute. If you move it, they won't hit it. They'll move away from it. They're hitting baits that they have stunned. That's just one of the many little wrinkles with a surface lure that you have to keep in mind."

The veteran angler cited an example of what he often sees on Lake Okeechobee: bass feeding on mosquito minnows.

"They're a small bait, not much bigger than freshwater shrimp," he said. "They will get in thick grass and bass will run through there and spook them.

"When they shower (in panic), they get on top of that grass and bass will turn around and grab them. They will eat them right off the grass. That's when a small profile bait will work."

But other times, fish will hit with their mouths closed. "They're just mean fish," he said. "Sometimes they will eat and sometimes they won't."

Sam added that he's seen dead shad floating on the water, killed by bass. "But they were so full that they couldn't get another one down their throats," he said. "But the predator part of their brains was still saying 'kill it.'

"Those little green fish are just plumb mean. You know that. After you've been catching fish, just look at your thumb."

Field Testing

Sam learned about what makes a good topwater bait by logging in thousands of hours at his 448,000-acre laboratory known as Lake Okeechobee. And he did that not just as a lure designer, but as a guide for decades, eager to teach his customers how to catch bass, as well as treat them to a great time on the water.

"I will keep baits tied on longer if I like what I see there," he said about field testing his lures. "When you're trying to create a new concept in a surface lure, how it acts when you throw it out there the first time is how it's gonna act if you throw it 10,000 times more.

"It doesn't take but a couple of casts to see if it's gonna work like you want it to or not," he added.

"What I do is take a piece of wood. I will seal it with three coats of lacquer. I put hooks on it and usually put a series of holes on the belly."

A sealed bait, like a painted bait, won't take on water, which would change the action, Sam explained.

"Then I throw it out there and see what it does. I also tinker around with belly hook to adjust the weight and see how much the tail goes down and the head goes up.

"Sometimes, I wind up making a two-hook bait into a three-hook bait so it floats right," he said.

"I use as big a treble hook as I can that still will allow the bait to do what I want it to do. If it's too big, I use a smaller hook. That's why the Rat-L-Trap has a bigger hook on the belly and a smaller on the tail."

The lure designer added with a laugh that "people who tinker are the worst people to sell baits too because they have preconceived ideas of what that bait should do.

"But it's their idea, not mine. I tell them to do whatever they want to do with the bait. But if they want it to do what I designed it to do, then they need to leave it like it is."

The native Floridian said that he learned early on that adding paint to the baits doesn't noticeably change the action which is why he doesn't bother for those he is field testing.

Part II: Bass and Baits

"I've caught more fish with unpainted baits than painted baits," he revealed. "I've sold a few too. But mostly they're too bland for fishermen."

How can it be that be that plain baits work so well? Doesn't the color and/or color pattern of a lure matter to the fish?

"I'll let you know when I get to Heaven," Sam said.

10. Let's Catch Some Little Green Fish

Here's how you do it on topwater, according to Sam:

"It's not the number of casts you make in a day, but the placement of your lure and the attention you give your lure that are most important. Let the fish help you determine the best method.

"After the lure impacts the water, watch it and the area around it for signs of movement. If you see action, but the cast does not produce a strike, try again in the same area. Continue casting until you think that there isn't any interest from the fish.

"A wake behind the lure usually means you are working it too fast, or maybe the fish just doesn't have enough interest to strike. Work the lure slower for a few more casts. Then, if the bass still doesn't strike, change to another type of surface lure in a smaller size. If the fish still doesn't react, move on, but remember the spot and return later to give it another try.

"If the fish boils just after you remove the lure from the water, it can mean it is holding in deeper water under your boat or it may have followed the lure out from your original target. Try moving your boat farther from the bank, grass edge, or the underwater cover you are fishing.

"Keep your mind on the job at hand and learn to look for any sign of fish movement in your line of sight. If you're thinking of anything but fishing, then you're not fishing right and you could miss bites."

Right Tool for the Job

In terms of fishing line for topwater baits, Sam prefers 15-pound monofilament.

"It's stiff enough that it won't override and get caught in the hooks and props," he explained. "Line lighter than that gets limp and gets tangled."

Topwaters can have a predisposition to catch in hooks because the bait "doesn't stop just because you stop pulling," he explained. "And if the bait overrides the line, it can cost you good fish."

An additional way to prevent overriding is secure a bobber stopper or a small piece of rubber to your line. Then slide on about an inch of a WD-40 tube or coffee stirrer, before tying the line to the bait.

"You also can take a rubber band and tie granny knots on the line," Sam added. "That makes a rigid spot without putting a knot in the line. It's not pretty, but it works.

"And if you think that it's too ugly, just think what a hook looks like hanging on a bait."

The Retrieve

For Sam, the topwater retrieve that provokes the most strikes is two jerks and a twitch.

"I do that about 85 percent of the time," he explained. "But watch the fish, and they will tell you how hard to jerk. And that can change over the course of a day."

That's because of sun movement across the sky. "Light penetration changes as time passes," the luremaker explained, adding that overhead sun makes it easier for fish to see you, your boat, and other dangers.

"Fish are always cautious and conscious of the danger of birds feeding on them. It's a natural protective mode," he said.

That's why bass often will be more aggressive when the sun is lower. A little ripple can help with that too. "It distorts everything and hides you and your line," Sam said.

Whatever retrieve you're using, hold you rod tip up when reeling in slack, Sam advised. "That makes the line go straight to the plug and keeps the bait from turning over and over and kinking your line.

"If you hold the rod tip down, especially with prop baits, the bait will turn over and the line will twist."

The Hookset

The belly hook on a topwater bait catches most of the bass, Sam believes. Still, fish will strike the tail, often attracted by the sparkle and subtle movement of a Mylar skirt.

When that happens, "Don't set the hook hard," he warned. "Just snug him.

"The fish is going to turn his head sideways when he hits the bait. It's a natural reflex, especially when he feels the hook. When that happens, the other hooks will get stuck in his mouth too."

In fact, Sam advises the "snug set" for even explosive strikes.

"You have to let 'em have it," he said. "Your human brain reacts and you want to jerk, and you're a lot faster than you think you are when you react.

"But you have to let the fish eat the bait. When it disappears, then you snug him."

Sometimes, though, you can't put a hook into the bass because it's a "junkyard dog fish.

"They're just plumb mean," Sam explained. "They will try to kill the bait by hitting it with their mouth shut. I've seen 'em come out of the water and come down on a bait with their mouth shut."

Sam recalled visiting the lab of Paul Schafland, the fisheries biologist primarily responsible for the state's successful peacock bass introduction program in South Florida canals. Schafland determined that the predatory peacocks would help control dozens of illegally introduced exotic fish species, while not damaging the largemouth bass fishery.

"He had a bass in a tank and then he put another one in there," Sam remembered. "That first fish would run into the other's stomach and try to kill him. I mean, he was just mean.

"You can see it during a frenzy bite, when you catch doubles. They're trying to get the bait out of the other fish's mouth. They're trying to get that drumstick."

In summing up the vast difference between topwater bites, Sam said, "I've been out there and all of a sudden — where's my bait!? I'll pull on it and a fish has got it and I didn't even see him take it. They can be just like a vacuum cleaner. They open that mouth and suck everything in.

"Other times, I've had them hit so hard that they knocked the paint off the bait. The bass is just a mean fish."

Topwaters for Tournaments?

"Yes," said Sam.

"If it's a bait he has confidence in, a topwater will contribute to a tournament angler's bag. Between 10 and 2, he's liable to get a big fish.

"An awful lot of fish are caught in tournaments on topwater baits, and the angler won't tell people what he is doing," he said. "The only way that the secret gets out is if his co-angler tells."

Many competitors will put a limit in the boat with other baits and then go after a "kicker" with a topwater, the lure-maker added.

Although the bait is not one of his, Sam said the Zara Spook is one of the most popular topwaters among tournament anglers. "That's one of the better walking baits and it has been for generations," he added.

"I could make a bait exactly like that and it would work just as well. But it wouldn't have 'Zara Spook' on it and, therefore, it wouldn't sell."

11. Bass in the Big O

Lake Okeechobee is noted more for producing quality bass in good numbers than double-digit trophies. Still, your chances of catching a 10-pound-plus largemouth are better in this massive body of water than in most of the nation's bass fisheries.

A couple of years ago, one of Sam's friends took a double-digit on top just a few yards from us. My biggest there weighed 8-8 and I caught it with Sam, of course. I've also caught quite a few 6's and 7's.

Sam's largest weighed 10-4, and he estimated that he's taken a half dozen fish weighing 10 or more on topwater baits, as well as "a bunch of 9's."

Some sources claim the unofficial lake record is 15-5. By contrast, Florida's state record is 17-4 (17.27 pounds). Sam recalled that the largest bass he has seen on the Big O weighed 14-8. It was caught on a topwater in 1952 and weighed on meat scales.

One of his most memorable catches occurred during the late 1960s at Cochran's Pass, when he caught a dozen doubles consecutively on a crankbait. Then he landed two or three singles, before taking five more doubles in a row.

During his decades of pursuing bass on Lake Okeechobee, Sam has learned that it contains "two strains, resident dwellers and lake roamers.

"From June to November, I'm catching mostly resident fish. They stay on the grasslines all the time," he explained.

"You really can't keep up with the lake roamers (in open water).

"Lake roamers are gypsy fish. I tell people that you could go out there, make four casts and catch four 10-pounders in a spot, if you were lucky. Then you could go back there to that same spot for the next 10,000 years and never get another bite because they're not going to stay there. They're following food."

But starting possibly as early as October, the larger population of lake roamers start joining resident fish in the marshes. "During the spawn cycle, they all come to the vegetation, if there's any available," Sam said, referring to the fact that extended periods of high, dark water can diminish grassbeds and, by extension, bedding areas.

"From about November through April, the population of larger bass doubles in the aquatic grass areas," he added. "Sometimes the spawning cycle can even last seven or eight months."

If you're catching bass in and around the grass during this time, you can tell whether you've caught a resident bass or a roamer by its color, Sam pointed out. "Resident dwellers are greener, with a little yellow cast to them. Sometimes, they're almost black, like in Fisheating Creek, where they have a black hue to them."

By contrast, roamers generally are lighter colored.

Where to Find Bass

In Lake Okeechobee, fish generally are near aquatic vegetation. But this shallow-water lake that's spread across

Part II: Bass and Baits

730 square miles and is nearly 36 miles long boasts seemingly endless areas of "fishy" looking habitat.

In general, the southern part of the lake, from Belle Glade to Clewiston is the best to fish year around, according to Sam. He attributes that to deeper water and an organic muck bottom, over limestone. "It's not mud. It's muck, and it's firm," he said, adding that manmade structures such a rim canals and barrow pits also are assets.

The latter were dug to extract lime rock for roadbeds around the lake.

Additionally, a fish-holding reef runs all the way from Observation Island on the west to Pahokee on the east.

"The area is especially better in summer than anyplace else in the lake," he added. "There's more water depth, and big fish don't have to go out as far into the lake as they do in other places that have sand and rock bottom. Muck doesn't erode like sand. Muck retains itself.

"As a rule of thumb, for every 100 yards you travel, you will get 6 inches deeper."

Additionally, the west side, from Clewiston to Okeechobee on the north end, provides the best aquatic vegetation for spawning. "You have grass that grows way out into the lake basin," the luremaker said.

"You have Moonshine Bay on the back side (west), along with Turner's Cove and Cochran's Rocks, on the north side of Observation Island," he added.

"Observation Island is a natural island, a sand island. And you've got the shoal itself, where willow bushes are, with shallow water there. That's where wave action during lower lake levels washes everything in there. That's the biggest spawning area. That means, in wintertime, that part of the lake is the best."

By contrast, the least productive area generally is on the lower east side, north of Pelican Bay.

Notable Names

In case you're wondering about some of those names that Sam mentioned and others that you've heard about:

"There was a still out there in the flats at the turn of the century (20th), in what we now call the **Cow Pasture**," Sam said in explaining how **Moonshine Bay** came by its label.

Coincidentally, the Big O also boasts a second landmark tied to the illegal whiskey trade.

"We have a Bear Beach and a **Bare Beach**," Sam said. "Bear refers to animals. Bare refers to a beach with nothing on it, and it's between Clewiston and South Bay on U.S. 27."

On this beach "with nothing growing on it," he recalled, "moonshine was stashed. Bootleggers with Model T's, they knew where it was buried and they picked it up and delivered it. This was during Prohibition."

Turner's Cove, meanwhile, "was named for Mr. Turner. He was a commercial fisherman who anchored his houseboat in the area."

MacMillan Cross on the reef at the lake's south end is one of the more recent landmarks, Sam said. "It was named for two individuals who died of hypothermia.

The Monkey Box is one of the best known landmarks on Lake Okeechobee, but many don't know how it got its name.

"They washed up on the reef. Just because it's Florida doesn't mean you can't die of hypothermia."

The veteran angler added that the reef has a natural pass through it known as **Hole-in-the-Wall**.

The lake's west side, meanwhile, boasts the **Monkey Box**.

"The west side had a railroad, but Clewiston didn't have a road going to it," Sam said. "They dug a channel out of Moore Haven to carry mail and to bring fish and produce in by boat, and at the end of the 7-mile canal they put a beacon light.

"Over time, they quit using the channel as a thoroughfare, and the beacon light got in disrepair. After that, a monkey-faced owl used to roost in it. My father told me that. He came here in 1921 and beacon light was functioning then."

Finally, some islands, such as **Ritter** and **Kramer**, were named for those who farmed on them. "They diked them off and grew vegetables out there," Sam said.

"You could have 20-degrees temperatures and they wouldn't have any frost because of the dikes and the warmness of the water. They wouldn't lose their crops, while everything on the shore would be bone dead because of the cold."

12. Wind Can Be Your Friend

Sam Griffin likes the wind. "You want a little, at least a slight ripple," he said. "It breaks up the surface.

"Fish are always conscious of birds trying to feed on them.

"Also, if it's flat calm and you're casting to a bank, fish can see it and that spooks them even before your lure hits the water. A little ripple disguises that."

Additionally, that wind actually can produce "tides" that attract fish in large, shallow-water lakes such as Okeechobee.

"The harder the wind, the higher the tide," Sam explained. "Usually it happens in water not over 20 feet deep, and the fluctuation typically is no more than 6 inches. But pressure builds from the wind and creates a current that stimulates fish."

The pressure can build not only in boat lanes, but in sloughs, between cypress trees, and along creek channels and roadbeds.

The way the vegetation is leaning can tip you off to which way the currents are flowing. Most often, fish will face into the current, just as they do in rivers, looking for bait to come from that direction.

While a ripple can be helpful for fishing and moderate breezes can produce beneficial currents, white-capping waves are no reason to put away topwater lures.

"If it's really bad, if you've got waves coming up over the hull, you're gonna leave that situation," Sam said. "But if you're got a situation that you can handle, you can fish a topwater the length of a wave, so the bait rides up and on it each time and you're not pulling it into the wave or over the wave.

"You actually can see a fish when it hits your lure. And the wave will mirror that fish so it usually looks twice as big as it is."

Of course, do not throw overhand into the wind, even if it's blowing into your face from a grassline that you want to fish. Mostly all you will get for your trouble are backlashes. Fishing it from the side, allowing your bait to ride on the waves, might work.

But Sam suggested, "If it's windblown bad, give it up and go to the lee side of something. You'll do better."

Besides heavy wind making casting difficult, it also disturbs fish. "Fish will back off (rocks) or go back in (grass)," he said.

One of the biggest problems with fishing in the wind is the bow that it puts in your line.

"You can't always control that," Sam said. "And it's impossible to fish spinning tackle in the wind because you get such a big belly. Also, the bait will run in a big curve coming back to you. That makes it difficult to be effective."

The veteran angler's preferred tactic is to make a hard, strong cast, feathering the spool, laying out the line so that it doesn't develop that troublesome bow. "With a baitcaster, you can do that," he said.

Keeping your casts short also can help.

"If I'm fishing lily pads with a 15 miles per hour wind, I have to have accuracy," he said. "I have to hit the holes that I'm supposed to hit."

To do that, he will make casts of 15 to 20 feet, or sometimes even shorter. "I'll let the lure sit, then twitch it once or twice," he said. "And then I'll try to jerk it into the next pocket.

"You don't want to reel it (lure)," he cautioned. "You want to pop it with the rod and try to hit the next hole."

A similar same tactic can be used with needle grass, when it's straight up, Sam explained.

"You want a bait like a Florida Shad, which has a wider body in the middle," he said. "The bait will hit the grass and push it away before the hooks hit it. Bulrushes are the same way.

"Pitch it up in there, but don't start jerking. You have to finesse it. Ease it around.

"A slender bait will get hung up," Sam added. "But a wider, fatter bait will work."

When he was guiding, Sam sometimes cut off the lead hooks to make the baits more weedless for customers to counteract problems caused by wind and inability to cast accurately.

"But the problem with doing that is the lead hook catches about 75 percent of your fish," he said.

13. Trailing the Fish

Boat trails play a key role not just for anglers but for bass among the thousands of acres of marshes that dominate the Big O.

"Boat trails are good not only for running your boat, but fish will bed in them," Sam said. "Also, in the fall, mouths of those boat trails are just like the mouths of creeks, and you can sometimes get a bite or two in them."

The luremaker explained that good spawning habitat is created in the trails as motors run them, disturbing bottom sediment, which suspends. Then wave action parts it and pushes it out.

"That actually makes a little hump on each side that cultivates aquatic growth really well," Sam said. "It's like making a garden. You're creating habitat, with spawning areas just inches away in the boat trails."

If the adjacent grass is thin, the retired guide added, he might move out into it and throw across the trails.

"With topwater lures, I'll let it sit—one, two, three—and then jerk it twice," he explained. "I'll let it sit some more, jerk it twice, and let it sit.

"If they boil under it, I'll twitch it. Sometimes, they'll come back and eat it, and sometimes they won't. Sometimes, they just want to kill it because they're mean fish."

Boat trails aren't always good, he cautioned, and, often some parts will be good and others won't.

"If you find a little sweet spot, slow down," he said. "And don't be afraid to throw just about anything—a jig with a crawdad, soft plastic swimbaits, jerkbaits, and even shallow-running crankbaits if you're a good caster."

Trails are often Sam's go-to places in fall. "Those are the dog days, when it's tough catching fish anywhere," he said. "I'll fish the mouths of the trails and fish 'em in about 100 feet.

"I'll also fish openings on the lakefront, where you have current flow," he added. "That's current flow created mostly by the wind. It blows water in, and then, when it lets off, the water runs back out.

"That does two things. It generates a good bite and also helps keep the bottom clean, so grasses like hydrilla don't totally take over."

When the wind is especially gusty, as in a summer storm, it actually can rip up some of that grass. In the aftermath, it might suspend and eventually sink or it might form mats, good for pitching and flipping.

"Anglers will punch it with 1-ounce or 2-ounce lead," Sam said.

Coots also help with creation of those fish-holding mats.

"We've got a big coot population on Okeechobee in the winter," he said. "Coots dive down and pull up roots of grass to eat. Then the wind rolls up the grass into mats on the sides of cattails.

"Or they can suspend and get in windrows. Then you fish between the mats just like you'd fish boat trails, using topwaters.

"You can't cross fish them or you'd stay hung up," he said, adding that winter mats deteriorate more slowly than do those in summer.

In winter, mats over submerged hydrilla beds can be especially good for big fish. "They like to get in that thick stuff," Sam said. "That's their jackets, their blankets, their heating pads. They will lie in there and stay warmer.

"That's why flipping can be so good in the winter on Okeechobee. Those fish aren't out foraging for food. They're more dormant and trying to stay warm. What you get flipping is a reactionary bite."

The back side of a cold front, with a rising barometer, can make them even more inactive, he cautioned. "We can feel a temperature change. They can feel a pressure change.

"We think that fish hide in cover and behind structure to feed. They also do it to rest."

Hydrilla

But given a choice, Sam would vote "no" for hydrilla in Lake Okeechobee.

"I don't like hydrilla. It builds mud on the bottom and interferes with the spawn cycle of all fish," he said.

"Does it hold fish? Yes. Do I catch fish out of hydrilla? Yes. But I prefer it not be there. We caught a whole lot of fish in Lake Okeechobee before it was ever there. You still would. But it's impossible to get rid of it. That's been proven many times."

Hydrilla is a mud builder, he emphasized, because it grows so fast and tops out, blocking sun from reaching plants below, which die, sink to the bottom, and rot.

"Cattails are just as bad, maybe worse," Sam said. "They grow out of the water and have a lot of bulk."

Boat trails play a key role for fish and fishermen alike on Lake Okeechobee.

The retired guide added that he fishes hydrilla in much the same way that he does other grasses. He will throw topwaters in the holes and along the edges or punch through it with weighted soft plastics.

"Hydrilla came to Okeechobee between 1962 and 1965," Sam said. "The first time I saw it was close to a couple of boat ramps. That tells you where it came from. It came from trailers. But before that, I don't know."

Fishing the Lines

Along with boat trails and mats, Sam focuses his efforts on fishing the "hard" and "soft" lines of Lake Okeechobee's marshes and edges.

"A hard line is a bank of cattails or reeds or any other thick bank with open water right up to it," he explained.

"You might have hyacinths, smart weeds, or grass against it, stuff that's really thick on top, but nothing underneath because it's not imbedded on the bottom. Fish don't penetrate it. They don't go into the cattails."

Instead, he added, "Fish are roaming, patrolling. They've got deep water close to them so they can escape there from a predator comes along."

Those predators can include birds, gators and even... "Big catfish will eat a bass. They'll eat anything, including topwater baits," Sam said. "I've caught channel catfish up to 22 pounds on topwater baits."

The luremaker likes to throw popping baits on hard lines because they're easier to keep in the strike zone for a longer time. "The forward motion is reduced when you're working it," he said. "It doesn't come forward to you as fast as a single-prop bait."

And you should keep your eyes on the bait as you retrieve it, not looking for where you want to cast next, he added.

"If you see a boil when you lift the bait out of the water, it's telling you something. You're working your bait too fast. They're following it out, and, when you're reeling in the last 10 or 15 feet, they're chasing it. Sometimes they'll even hit it. Other times they won't. You need to slow it down."

Also, you might try dragging the lure in a figure 8 alongside the boat. "Bass are similar to muskie in that regard," Sam said. "Snook and tarpon are similar. So are peacock bass."

Sam recalled fishing with a guide party along a hard line with smart weed edge, behind a duo competing in a tournament.

"I'm coming behind them and catching fish," he said. "They weren't catching anything because the fish weren't in that grass."

Slopes are a variation of hard lines, and bass like to travel up and down them, Sam explained.

"If you're in a canal and see rocks protruding out of the bank, that's where the canal was dug, and you have an erratic slope, which makes it good," he said. "But if you have grass growing out, especially something like torpedo grass, the water may not be 6 inches deep at the end of the grass. That means a slow tapering bank, and that's not good. Faster tapers usually hold more fish.

Part II: Bass and Baits

"You can go down banks and almost figure out where fish will be from that reason alone. Faster tapers hold more fish."

By contrast, soft lines are characterized by grasses such as pepper, ribbon, and hydrilla that fish can penetrate.

"With those, you want to fish slower," Sam said. "Look for holes or even where it gets thicker. Find those special places that fish may want to be, and that's usually anything that's different.

Of the two types of joint grass, the smaller, wiry variety usually is better. "It grows thicker on the top, but doesn't have as much bulk underwater as the big stem," he said.

"Sometime you can float a topwater along that and catch fish. Other times, not. I can't explain why fish do what they do," Sam added.

Pepper grass with bulrushes, meanwhile, creates a prime soft line. "That's the best you can get. Pepper grass will hold baitfish," he said.

"With bulrushes, you want some thickness, at least in pods. You don't want a bunch of thin stuff, unless it's a spawning area. Then that's okay because they spawn on root system."

He added that bass typically won't spawn in bulrushes that front open water. "They prefer 30 or 40 feet behind the thicker stuff," he said. "They want some protection for their beds.

"You might think a bass is dumb," Sam laughed. "But it has sense enough to know where to bed. And enough sense to fool us."

14. Lost and Found

By Art Hodges

(Art Hodges is a guide on Lake Okeechobee.)

Several years ago I received a phone call from an FLW tournament director on the last day of a tournament on Lake Okeechobee. He asked me if I could go out on the lake to tow in a pro who had called in with an motor problem.

It was very close to weigh-in time, and the director was a little brief with me, when he provided the location of the boat. He told me it was just off Horse Island, and I thought it would be easy to find. I asked a couple of questions, which he could not answer. When I told him I had a GPS, he gave me the numbers.

Well Sam Griffin has one too. At the time of the call I had just pulled into the Clewiston Walmart parking lot, site of the weigh-in. I live several miles away in Moore Haven and, of course, my boat was at home. I decided the quickest way to get the job done was to call Sam.

Well, you know Sam. His answer was sure. "Let the man know I'm on my way," he said.

Some time passed before I had the opportunity to talk with the director again, because he was preparing to start the weigh-in.

Within an hour I got a call from Sam, informing me he had been as far north of Horse island as Indian Prairie Canal and there were no boats anywhere in sight. He added that he would head offshore, going back south to see if the boat was beyond eye sight from where he made his run north. With sunset getting close. I finally caught the tournament director at a free moment and told him the situation described. He said to me, "Well, your guy must be lost."

I told him, "Your pro may be lost but I promise you that there is no way Sam Griffin would ever be lost on Lake Okeechobee."

GPS is better known to Sam's friends, locals, and pros alike as the Griffin Positioning System, and he found the guy pretty much in the middle of the lake.

I was told that it was after dark when they finally got the guy's boat loaded. Since he couldn't get the boat up on pad, they had to idle into Harney Pond and then relocate his trailer from Clewiston to Lakeport.

That fisherman with the broken down boat was rescued by a *real pro*, and I'm not talking about just Sam's navigation and fishing ability. He is a gentleman, always ready and willing to help others.

Part III
The Man, The Myth,
The Legend

15. Super Cool Poppy!

By Katelyn Fabian

(Sam Griffin named a crankbait that he designed "Lil' Katie" in honor of his granddaughter.)

Of course, many of my memories with Sam Griffin are filled with fishing…

Like casting off the back dock for bream with little pieces of bread as bait, the tournament I once fished with him that I could never forget, or convincing him to let me paint bright pink lures in his shop.

But for me, he has always just been my Poppy. As much as I have always loved him, it wasn't because of his unmatched knowledge of Lake O or the fact that he never fails to catch more bass than whoever is out on the boat with him on any given day. More so because of his endless supply of chocolate ice cream, letting me pretend to drive his boat, and playing school with me. Not to mention he has one of the kindest, biggest hearts of anyone I know, and I've been lucky enough to be on the receiving end of his love for the last 23 years.

As I've grown up, I've begun to realize how truly special (and super cool!!) my Poppy is. Last year, after he was inducted into the Freshwater Fishing Hall of Fame, we threw a big party to celebrate his amazing and well-deserved achievement. It was a blast and more than 200 people showed up to honor him. Some people I knew, many I didn't, but every single person bragged on my Poppy. Every. Single. One.

Granddaughter Katelyn fished a bass tournament with Sam in 2013, and has since gone on to catch other species of fish, including tarpon.

Not only is he a legend in the fishing community, but he has made a lasting impact on those around him. Many people told me stories about how he and Nana opened up their home to them in a time of need, how he taught them everything they know about fishing, how loving, humble, and charismatic he is and has always been.

Part III: The Man, The Myth, The Legend

As many people know, Poppy loves to tell a good story. But it was so heart-warming to hear people speak so kindly in their stories about him.

I've always seen him through the eyes of a grand-daughter with love, respect, and lightheartedness. But since that party, I have a new level of admiration and thankfulness for him. He's not just my grandpa, but an extremely hardworking, loving, funny, smart, family man who continuously puts others first and does the right thing.

Everything that he has accomplished he has earned, all with a smile on his face and a Snickers in his pocket. Everyone should aspire to be more like Sam Griffin.

16. Turkey Bacon and the Twinkie Diet

When he takes friends fishing, Sam often shares his Twinkie diet with them.

Dave Burkhardt's first fishing trip with Sam Griffin was a "white-knuckle experience."

"When we climbed in the boat, it was dark and foggy," he remembered. "Sam started the boat and idled out a ways.

"Then he hit the gas and I thought, 'How in the Hell does he know where he's going?'"

More than 20 years and many fishing trips later, Dave no longer worries about where Sam is taking him on Lake Okeechobee on dark and foggy mornings or any other time.

"That first trip made a lasting impression on me," he said. "Sam knows this lake better than anyone. How he knows it as well as he does is beyond me. But he knows what kind of vegetation is where. He knows every turn through the marshes. He knows the bottoms and where the fish spawn.

"And as big as that lake is, he always knows where he is. Conditions, depth, temperature, he has it all dialed in."

Besides the two being fishing buddies, Sam field tests fishing line for Dave, owner of Trik Fish line company in Clermont, Fla. And in return, Dave, who usually prefers soft plastics, has caught more than a few bass on Sam's baits, especially when fishing the Big O.

Sam teaching him how to properly fish the Lil' Richard and other lures in aquatic grass played a big role in that.

"I was looking at him bringing his bait through there (vegetation) and thinking that it looked impossible," Dave said. "What I learned is that you have to watch which way the wind is coming from, and you can't quarter off.

"You can fish the thick stuff if you make the wind your friend and cast with it. The wind makes alleys through stuff like reeds so you can get your bait through it."

Away from the water, meanwhile, Sam introduced Dave to turkey bacon.

"I'd never had it before," Dave recalled. "Now, whenever I see or smell it, it puts a smile on my face because it reminds me of Sam and going fishing."

What does turkey bacon have to do with fishing? When you're Sam's friend, he doesn't just take you fishing and show you how to catch topwater bass, he also just might invite you to spend the night at his place, where he prepares breakfast, as well as lunches for the boat.

Honey buns were a staple of those lunches for years. But then the doctor told Sam that he needed to lower his cholesterol.

"He followed his doctor's orders and switched to Twinkies," Dave said, adding that Sam did, indeed, lower his cholesterol with the switch.

"Now I look forward to Twinkies," he added.

Along with good fishing and tasty meals, a visit with Sam provides something even more important, his long-time friend said. As an example of what he means, he recalled a time when Sam found a large and hungry concentration of fish. The two stood up front, catching bass on nearly every cast, while their mutual friend, Larry Thornhill, refused to join in the fun.

He could have picked up one of Sam's or Dave's rods and caught fish too. But he had brought along some new, hollow rods, which required that line be threaded up through them, and he was determined to rig them up and use them, no matter how long it took.

"Trying to get that line through the rods was liking trying to push a rope," Dave said. "Larry was cussing and fussing.

"And Sam was incredulous. He just couldn't understand how anyone could sit on the back deck and get frustrated while we were catching fish and having fun.

"But Larry was an engineer and bull-headed, while Sam is easy-gong with a good sense of humor," he continued. "It was a yin and yang type of thing, and I think that Sam had his head in the right spot about what was important."

Of his good friend, Dave added, "Sam is like a guy in the military who has your back. And whatever he says, you can believe. He's positive on things and friends, and people in general. I've never heard him say a negative thing about anyone. I've never heard him say an angry word.

"I wish that I could be more like Sam."

17. National Recognition

In December 2019 more than 200 people attended a celebration to honor Sam's induction into the Freshwater Fishing Hall of Fame.

One of those was Charles Davis, the man who nominated him. Davis, an avid lure collector, collaborated with Bill Stuart, who provided a biography of Sam that he wrote for a 1996 book entitled *Florida Lure Makers and Their Lures: A History, Identification, and Relative Value Guide Book.*

"Everyone thinks the world of Sam, and a lot of people know him," Davis said.

Davis, who formerly worked at Anheuser-Busch in Jacksonville, first learned about Sam during the 1980s, when a friend gave him one of the luremaker's baits.

"I love to fish topwaters, and I got hooked on them," he continued. "I called Sam to order lures and then started calling him to give reports on how I was doing with them."

As their friendship grew, Charles and Sam fished together twice on Lake Okeechobee.

"Sam never made a bad lure," Charles said.

Here's what the Hall of Fame said in announcing Sam's enshrinement:

"**Sam Griffin (Florida)** was born in 1937 and was 15 years old when he carved his first lure. He used guava wood because he knew it would float. When the lure hit the water it immediately sank and that was the beginning of his experimentation, creating lures that caught big fish. His initial offerings included the Old Line Sides lure which is coveted today by collectors. His other early experiments yielded the Hobo.

Charles Davis nominated Sam for membership in the Fresh Water Fishing Hall of Fame.

"In 1989 when Griffin sold all the rights of Griffin Lures to Luhr-Jensen, they were producing six of his creations. They were Sammy Shad, Wobble Pop, Bass Baffler, Lil' Chris, Jerk'n Sam, and Nippin' Sam. Griffin tested his lures on Lake Okeechobee, where he guided for over 50 years."

Part III: The Man, The Myth, The Legend

The following excerpt from Stuart's history of Sam and his lure business details his involvement in local politics and other activities:

"Sam was active in Glades County politics. He was elected to the County Commission in 1980 and served for seven years and as chairman in 1986. As one might expect, his main interest revolved around the lake and the county's use of it as a major resource.

"He saw to it that beacon lights were placed at the entrance to each channel, and he was the driving force behind providing adequate ramps and parking and access to the lake. As a result of his work, they now have three double ramps and over five acres of parking.

"In 1983, he was invited to serve as a director of the Harold DeTar Fly Fishing Tournament. Harold, a retired public relations man, started the tournament in 1956 for outdoor writers and other media people to promote the lake and its fly fishing potential. Sam remained on the board until 1992

"Sam did a lot of tournament fishing until 1985, when he stopped to devote more time to his business. His wall of trophies and plaques were given by United Bass Fishermen, Fishfinders, B.A.S.S., and the Gator Division of Red Man. In 1975, he was the Clewiston Tournament Champion and, the same year, was selected Fisherman of the Year by the Southwest Lake Okeechobee Bass Club."

In recognition of the work Sam has done for the community and lake, Glade County Commissioner John

Ahern recommended that a proposed elevated boardwalk at Harney Pond Overlook Park be named in his honor.

"Sam Griffin is going to be inducted into the Fresh Water Fishing Hall of Fame," he said. "I thought we could do something, maybe name it in his honor. He's spent a lifetime on the lake and promoting the lake."

The previous overlook was taken down after being severely damaged by a hurricane.

When Sam was on the Glades County Commission, he joined other members riding donkeys at a local fund-raising event. Only Sam was so tall that the donkey stood between his legs.

18. My Guide in Fishing and Life

By Russell Echols

(Russell Echols guided with Sam and friends often referred to him as "the legend in training.")

Fishing with Sam is an amazing experience. It's world-class training and world-class therapy.

Sam uses fishing on Lake Okeechobee to teach bass patterns, the biology of the fish, and the ecological impacts he's noted, as well as life lessons and the importance of God in all of it.

Sam's boat is his church and I'm a better man than I ever could have been without him being my guide in fishing and my guide in life. Sam Griffin is a treasure!

Following are a couple of my favorite memories of our time together on the water: The first time that I fished with Sam was at a ProCraft owners tournament on Lake Toho in the late 80's. The chance to fish with the Legend was exciting and I really felt the pressure. At the time, I had three rods and reels and not much tackle. But Sam said not to worry because he would have plenty.

We loaded up and off we went on the 2 1/2-hour drive for a day of pre-fishing Friday before the tournament. About daylight, we were unloading at the ramp when I heard Sam yell, "Oh, no!"

113

He had taken his tackle boxes home to reorganize them, and forgotten to bring them.

"What are we gonna do?" I asked nervously.

He replied, "I got some of my old topwater plugs in the boat. We're gonna go fishing!"

And fish we did. We found two spots holding fish. We didn't try to catch them. We just let them explode on the plugs and knock them a foot in the air. Sam said," That's all we need to know."

The first day we weighed in about 15 or 16 pounds and sat about 25th place out of roughly 200 boats, with the leaders at 26 pounds. Sunday we caught another solid bag that put us a little over 30 pounds for the tournament and a respectable sixth place, just a few pounds out of first. We did that with six of Sam's old topwater plugs, including some that were prototypes that had no paint on them.

He never got flustered and never worried about a thing. He just calmly went fishing, and we caught a big bag of fish. It was a lesson in having confidence in yourself that serves me well to this day.

Later, when I was guiding with Sam , we booked some anglers from Tennessee who were repeat customers. Two days before the trip, we searched for a concentration of bass, which were shut down tight because of a cold front. The first day, we caught two fish, and it got worse the second. By 2 p.m., we hadn't had a bite.

Then Sam found a large hydrilla patch. We fished all around and tried several techniques, but to no avail. Finally, Sam picked up a plastic worm, cast it into the grass, and let it sit for what seemed like a minute before he barely moved it and felt a tap. But the fish never took the worm.

Nevertheless, Sam reeled in and said, "Let's go. We got 'em!"

I was stunned and replied, "We got 'em?"

He assured me that we did. He explained that the fish were cold and so they were covered up in this thick stuff. Tomorrow the lake would be warmer so fish would be more active, he added, and we'd have shiners for bait. During the next two days with the Tennessee anglers, we used five dozen shiners per boat and caught more than 100 bass out of a spot that wasn't 75 yards long. More than half of those bass were over 5 pounds. All six of the guide party caught a fish over 6 pounds, with the largest bass of the trip being well over 8 pounds.

No one but Sam has that kind of knowledge and feel for bass in the Big O.

19. Butterhead and the Zen of Fishing

By Crissy Fabian

(Crissy Fabian is Sam Griffin's daughter.)

Let me start this out by saying that fishing wasn't always a pleasure for me. As you can imagine, the four of us spent a fair amount of time as a family fishing when I was younger. While I always enjoyed the first hour or so, I got bored after awhile. I think my brother felt the same way, but that is his story to tell.

Fishing was always fun for a little bit, but we never shared the passion for it that my Dad has. He would never admit this, but he has to be a little disappointed. He never gives up trying, and, for this, I'm thankful.

As the years have gone by, I find myself really enjoying our time fishing together. Sure, I enjoy the sport of it and the thrill of the catch. But I am just now realizing what my Dad figured out all those years ago: fishing is surprisingly Zen. The sound of the water, the feel of the breeze, the smell of the grasses combined with plastic worms and fishing line, the repetitive movement of casting out and reeling in, the pleasure of time spent with a treasured loved one.

My Daddy loves to fish, but I think even more than that he loves getting others to enjoy fishing. Anyone who has had the pleasure of using my Dad's guiding services knows that he goes above and beyond to make sure all levels of fisher people have a great time.

As an adult, Crissy Fabian has discovered that fishing with her father is "surprisingly Zen."

This is pretty much my experience with my Dad: He packs a lunch, snacks, and drinks. He brings the sunscreen. He makes sure I wear a hat and fishing shirt so I don't get sunburnt. He gears up the rods and reels, shows me where to cast, coaches me on technique, and patiently unsnarls my many Level Orange backlashes, but first gives me a new outfit to use while he does this.

Part III: The Man, The Myth, The Legend

This courtesy extends to bathroom accommodations. I used to be able to "hang it over the side," but age and stage fright have made this a problem. So he brings along a bucket for my use now. For the very particular (my daughter), he will even make a special trip back to shore for a real bathroom break. It's the little things.

It's hard to condense so many memories to just one, so let me point out some highlights:

- Fishing in Moonshine Bay recently and the Monkey Box later that same day.
- Taking my daughter's friends out fishing and watching my Dad help them like he has helped me.
- Winning a camera for my big catch when I was about 10 (newspaper contest).
- My Dad's fishing and boating ingenuity (e.g., his stripper pole).
- Forgetting to release the parking brake when I pull the boat trailer out of the water: Every. Single. Time.
- Fishing tournaments with my Dad.

I love you, my Daddy!

From your Butterhead.

20. Only the Shadow Knows

By Troy Gibson

(Troy Gibson is an Arkansas tournament angler and, like Sam, a lure designer. He specializes in soft plastic baits and, among others, created Strike King's coffee-scented lures.)

While we were fishing on Lake Okeechobee, I asked Sam, "Where are these fish? They should be here."

Sam replied "Only the shadow knows."

I turned to look at him and he had the most pleasant smile on his face when I asked him what that meant.

He told me that God made fish and men with tails. He also said that, unlike men who sometimes sits on their tails, fish use them constantly and move all the time and the hunt is what really draws people to this sport. Anyone can catch bass but finding them is what is most important. During our years of fishing together, Sam has made other observations about fish and men, all of them helpful. But this one really made me a better professional fisherman.

I honestly think that when God allowed for Sam to be born that He was looking in a mirror because Sam Griffin is the truest to heart and helpful person I have ever met. He's not just that way to people he knows either, but to everyone he comes in contact with. He is always helping people and making sure, to the best of his ability, to do the right thing.

Big Sam and Big O

When you fish with him, he puts you in position to catch the fish, not him. He works so hard at making others happy that I sometimes wonder if he ever thinks of himself and his happiness. But I can answer that, because if you are happy, he is happy.

Sam Griffin is all that I want to be and, every day I meet someone, I reflect on Sam and try to do as Sam would. He says that faith, hope, and love always will get you through anything in this crazy world that we live in.

(Editor's note: During the golden age of radio, when Sam was a youngster, millions tuned in regularly to hear the adventures of The Shadow, a mysterious crime fighter also featured in pulp novels and magazines. "Who knows what evil lurks in the hearts of men? The Shadow knows" were the introductory words for the radio episodes.)

21. Pop's Perfect Swing

By Samuel J. Griffin

*(Samuel J. Griffin, known to many
as "Joe," is Sam Griffin's son.)*

I have so many great memories of my father. Before I go into any of them, I must disclose that, despite my Pop's best efforts, I did not turn out to be a very good fisherman. To be honest, I don't really enjoy it that much compared to my other pursuits.

I don't have a boat, and I don't even own any fishing equipment. I have some of his famous lures for keepsakes, and he has given me a generous supply to give to my friends and business clients.

Alas, I'm a golfer and wine connoisseur. Nobody saw that coming I assure you.

It has only been later in life, as I matured and accumulated my own experiences, that I began to appreciate fishing with my Dad for what it really is. Although I do enjoy fishing more than I used to, it is all about being out there on Lake Okeechobee with him. We talk about things we probably wouldn't discuss if we were not alone in the boat, out of earshot from everyone except God and mother nature!

I also enjoy learning more about fishing—and just a little more about him—every time we go out. I get to hear stories about him, his mom, my Grandpa Joe, my Uncle Richard, and others. All of the stories took place on the Big

O. On each trip, I admit, I must re-learn techniques and skills taught and re-taught to me by the Legend many, many times so patiently over the years. One particular skill took me more than 50 years to get the hang of, but more about that later.

One of my earliest memories of my Dad had nothing to do with fishing. I was 5 or 6 years old maybe. I had developed an infection and became very sick with an extremely high fever. I have a vague recollection of our family doctor making a house call. They took me to Hendry General Hospital in Clewiston that night. I do not recall how long I was in the hospital, but I do remember I was put on a special diet. I remember it being referred to as a "bland" diet. It was most definitely bland, and it didn't include anything a kid like me wanted to eat or drink for sure. I was miserable and wanted to go home.

On one of the days my Mom and Dad visited, he came to the room by himself and sat down next to me. I remember he looked over at the door then looked at me. Then out of his jacket pocket he pulled a can of Coca Cola. I went from miserable to happy instantly! I was one happy little red-head boy! I've never had a better refreshment. That's all; it was that simple—a father giving his son a little unauthorized treat. I will never forget it.

The next memory I'd like to share is one of my favorites. I am a golfer. My Dad is a fisherman. For many years, he has tried to teach me to fish, with some modest successes. Over the years, many have tried to teach me to golf, with a little more success. Perhaps I'm a bit more skilled than the average recreational golfer, since I can shoot scores in the low 80s and high 70s. As for fishing, as long as my Dad sets me up, I usually can catch a handful and, in rare times, I've hauled in a few big ones like a pro.

One day, my Dad went golfing with me. He had never played the game in his life as far as I know, and I don't think he's even been to a putt-putt course more than a couple of times. But he was game to try, and I was happy to introduce him to my sport. Like almost all beginners, he struggled hitting the ball. But we forged on and were having a good time.

One mistake beginners often make, and I still do, is to swing too fast. It makes sense, right? Swing faster and the ball will go farther. I tried to explain that wasn't the case and he should swing "easy."

Then it hit me! A good golf swing essentially has the same rhythm as a long cast, that cast you make when you need the lure to hit a spot a little farther away from the boat than the norm. A smooth rhythm with good extension back and through is required unless you want a massive back-lash.

The moment I said this to my Pop, I could see him gain confidence. He knew exactly what I meant and was ready to execute. He gripped the club and set up to the ball like I'd showed him. He took the club back nice and slow and long. Then he released the club like he'd been doing it all his life.

The golf ball proceeded on a pro trajectory, nice and high right down the middle of the fairway! I heard that oh-so-sought-after click/swoosh sound a golf ball makes when it's been struck right in the sweet spot of the club. I am not sure how he felt, but I'm pretty sure he liked it because he posed a little just like us good golfers do when we stripe one. It had to be satisfying.

As for me, I can't describe how good it made me feel to see him hit that ball so well after I gave him that little tip. He hit it with my old Callaway 7-wood, the "Heaven Wood." I haven't used it in years, but I have kept it as a memento of that day.

Finally, I'll end with a more recent story, an actual fishing story this time.

We were on one of our traditional after Thanksgiving Day fishing trips. As usual, we put in at the ramp at Harney Pond Canal down the road from my folks' house in Lakeport. Dad took us out to a spot where he thought we'd be able to catch some. If you know anything about him or have ever been fishing with him, you know that he surely knows how to find fish. And, if there are fish to be had, he surely knows what technique and equipment to use to bring them in. Topwater, plastic worms, you name it. He has the necessary arsenal of tackle, rods, and reels ready to go.

On this particular day, it looked like plastic-worm fishing was going to be the technique of the day. Well, plastic-worm fishing always has been a struggle for me. It requires patience and paying close attention to what is going on at the end of your line. Not exactly a strength of mine.

I always struggle to maintain the right rhythm. Every little bump seems like it is a fish. And, of course, when I think it's a fish, I try to jerk it out of the water. But on this day, for some unknown reason, I brought a version of me that was a bit calmer and less stressed than in years past. Whatever the reason, I was able to "be as one" with my plastic worm. The bumps did not get me all hyped up and launched into fast-swing mode.

Then it happened. There was a bump! The bump! The kind that just gets your spine tingling and heart pumping. I did not realize it at the time, but, without thinking, I did what my dad had been trying to teach me for more than 50 years. A kind of peace came over me. I just eased off, gave it a little, brought in a little slack, and set the hook. I nailed him!

I don't remember how big that bass was, but that didn't matter. Fifty years of patient training finally had clicked.

Now, I had managed to catch fish with a worm before, but it never felt like this. I felt totally in control and confident in what I was doing this time. I caught more fish, and, the more I caught, the easier it was to tell when a bump was a fish. To make matters even better, I was more excited when I got a bump, but I was still able to control myself.

The best part of the whole thing was to see my Dad grin. He is always encouraging that way. He really didn't have to say anything. I knew he was proud of his middle-aged son. I felt so good about being out on the Big O with him and about life in general. I think he might have picked up his pace a little, thinking I might have a slight chance of keeping up with him on the count.

Big Sam and Big O

That day will always be a very special one to me because it was one of those that exemplifies what a relationship between a father and son is all about.

I love you, Pop!

22. My First Topwater Bass

By Steve Ulman

This presentation set of Sam's baits is one of Steve Ulman's most prized possessions.

After Sarah and I retired and sold the farm in Minnesota, we moved to South Florida. It wasn't just anyplace in South Florida, but the south edge of Lake Okeechobee, where I intended to resume the catfishing that I left behind.

As lifelong Episcopalians, Sarah and I were happy to find St Martin's Episcopal Church in Clewiston, and, to my great good fortune, the Senior Warden was a fisherman named Sam Griffin.

Sam starts all visitors to St Martin's out with one of his handmade wooden fishing lures, painted in the colors of the Episcopal Church, no hooks included. At coffee hour after the service, Sam invited me to go fishing with him sometime. Of course, I was back the next Sunday, sitting in the very same pew, just hoping he hadn't forgotten his invitation. He didn't. I was elated to say the least!

By the time the appointed day arrived, I had done a little research on Google and eBay and knew that my new church friend was no ordinary fisherman but "The Legend of the Lake" and "Mr. Wood Lure."

Even though I was a little nervous, I felt ready because I had been collecting Johnson fishing reel memorabilia for more than 50 years and had a working model of virtually every reel that the company had made. I chose a 1968 Johnson Commander reel with fresh 10-pound mono and a 5-foot fiberglass Johnson rod. I was a little excited so I was at the ramp early, only to find Sam in the water and ready to go.

When we left the ramp in his 20-foot Bass Cat pushed by a 250 Mercury, I had the first thrill of many, in a day I'll never forget. Sam, being the gentleman he is, never said a thing about my equipment. He tied a Lil' Richard in black and white on my line without comment.

After a few casts, just as the sun came up over the famed Lake Okeechobee, I had my first topwater largemouth bass.

Part III: The Man, The Myth, The Legend

As Sam likes to say, "You'll never forget your first kiss or your first topwater bass."

Over the years, I have had the good fortune to fish with Sam on several occasions. He has made a few suggestions about equipment, and my Johnson Reels are now back in the display case where they belong and my line doesn't stretch when I set the hook with my medium heavy rod.

But one thing hasn't changed. I still clearly remember my first topwater bass, just as I do my first kiss.

* * * *

Having bought and sold several dozen horses over my lifetime, I once considered myself better than average at the art of the deal. But I've belatedly learned that my skills pale in comparison to that of my gentle, loving wife, Sarah.

As an example I offer the following:

When I first met Sam, Legend of the Big O, I looked up his handmade wooden bass fishing lures on eBay. Single lures sold from $10 to $25, depending on age and condition, with the older lures bringing the premium prices. This told me collectors were in the hunt.

I have collected Johnson reel memorabilia for many years because I knew the Johnson family growing up in Mankato, Minn., where their reels were made. Adding Sam's colorful lures to my collection would liven it up.

What I really wanted was a seven-lure set in a presentation glass dome. Sam must not have made many of these, as they were selling for more than $250 on eBay.

My birthday was coming and Sarah asked, as she had for the last 60 years, "What do you want for your birthday?"

This year, unlike the last 59, I had an answer ready and waiting. I wanted a presentation glass dome of Sam Griffin's lures.

I fully expected her to go on eBay and bid on one, the only set that was currently offered. But that's not what she did.

She went straight to the source and asked Sam to make her a set. Sam did and it travels with us in our 5th wheel camper, right next to my 1964 pink Johnson Princess fishing reel.

Life is good. Knowing Sam, Sarah got a sweet deal, without any dickering involved, and I learned later that my quilter wife left him speechless when she asked him what weight thread I should use with the lures.

23. Uncle Sammy, the Boat Builder

By Kathy Decker-Griffin

(Kathy Decker-Griffin is Sam's niece and the daughter of his brother, Richard.)

When Uncle Sammy started tournament fishing, my Dad started quoting him when he took me fishing for bass. He would tell me where the bass are likely to hang out and where I should cast my lure. Sometimes that worked, but they were much better at fishing than I was.

My Dad, Uncle Sammy, and my granddaddy took me fishing before I was 5 years old. They were so patient with me. They baited my hook and tried to teach me to do it myself. If I got tangled in the weeds or hung up in a tree, they stopped fishing and patiently, sweetly got me untangled. I remember how special I felt. I knew they loved me.

When my Dad couldn't take me duck hunting, Uncle Sammy did. I was so excited. He told me how to keep the gun pointed just in front of the duck before I pulled the trigger. When he showed me, he made it look so easy. Even though I missed every time, I had fun anyway. I think the reason Uncle Sam is a fisherman instead of a hunter is because fishing has always been more challenging to him.

Big Sam and Big O

He did more than guide and show people how to catch bass too. Our family business also involved growing sugarcane and he helped Dad with that.

One day after I came home from school, I made my usual trip down the road to Dad at Uncle Joe's Fish Camp. Dad said, "Come here. I want to show you something your Uncle Sam made."

When we got to the shop, I saw an implement that Dad could use on our farm. It looked like a plough, but it wasn't. It could dispense fertilizer and seeds.

Dad loved to brag on his little brother. Come to think of it, Dad bragged on me too. I sure do miss him.

Uncle Sam built other things too, including fiberglass fishing boats. We got to go for a ride in one of them. It was fun and, no, it didn't sink!

Because we lived in a small rural community, word got out about my uncle's ability to make boats. Before long, my English teacher and her husband wanted Uncle Sammy to help them build a fiberglass tri-hull catamaran so that they could sail around the world.

He helped them make their dream come true.

Finally, I have to tell you that during the tough, sad times in my life, my Aunt Carol and Uncle Sam were always there for me. They have always listened, prayed, and encouraged me to do the right thing. Their encouragement and love helped me keep on keepin' on.

Now that my immediate family members have all gone home to be with the Lord, they are even more special to me. They make a wonderful team! When Uncle Sammy "caught" Aunt Carol, he caught the catch of his life.

24. Sam and Huck

By Bryan Honnerlaw

(Bryan Honnerlaw is a fishing guide and tournament angler who lives near Sam and Carol Griffin in Moore Haven.)

Sam teaches Huck Honnerlaw how to make wooden topwater baits.

Big Sam and Big O

I moved to Florida about 20 years ago to be a fishing guide on Lake Okeechobee. I had always heard about this guy named Sam Griffin who made lures and was a legend around the lake.

I didn't get to meet him for years. But finally I was introduced to him by Dewayne Evans, a fishing buddy Sam had befriended.

I was lucky enough to also be befriended by Sam. I got to go fishing with him shortly thereafter, and he quickly showed me the value of his Lil' Richard prop bait while I was practicing for a tournament.

The next weekend I finished third, and several key fish came from his magic bait.

Through the years, our family has become very fond of Sam and Carol. They are like second grandparents to our children. Sam has taken my son Huck under his wing, and brings him over to his shop and teaches him to build baits. This has been a wonderful blessing that I know my son will remember and cherish forever.

There's another thing I have always loved about this guy: When people criticize me or laugh at me for running my boat in places that I shouldn't and that are hard to access to catch a little green fish, I can just smile at them and say, "I know a much older and wiser man than I who does the same thing quite often."

25. What I Admire Most About Sam

By Gary Jones

Without any doubt, what makes Sam a special friend is his character. I know of no other person who is so giving. Not only would he give you the shirt of his back, he would grow the cotton, weave the fabric, and sew it together.

In the many conversations I have had with Sam, I can never remember him raising his voice, showing anger, or swearing. Sam assures me he has a point where he can be pushed too far, and no man would want to see the wrath of his anger. He says he knows all those swear words, but chooses not to use them.

I'm sure I have tested his character many times.

I remember once when we were out fishing together and I hooked a large mudfish (bowfin). After fighting the fish and getting it to the side of the boat, I asked Sam if he had a pair or needle-nose pliers. Back where I come from, we would never think about lifting one of those slimy, toothy critters into the boat.

Sam reached to his belt and then handed me one of those fancy multi-tool, folding pliers. With the pliers in hand, I reached over the side of the boat, grabbed the line just above the fish, and reached towards the hook with the pliers.

Big Sam and Big O

The plan was to grab the hook, give it a quick twist, and release the fish. I had done this hundreds of times over the years and it had always worked like a charm.

But this time, just as I was about to grab the hook, the dang fish flopped, causing me to drop those fancy pliers into the lake.

"Oh, Sam, I'm sorry," I said.

Sam, with his soft southern drawl, replied, "That's okay. It's just part of fishing. Here, I got another pair of pliers."

This time, he handed me a pair of needle-nose pliers and once again I grabbed the line, intending to release the fish.

Well, wouldn't you know it? Just as I grabbed the hook, the mudfish flopped again and I dropped the second pair of pliers into the lake.

By then, I was feeling like a complete ass.

But Sam looked and me and simply said, "Well, you are on your own now. I'm out of pliers."

The fish was released with a hook in its mouth and Sam and I went home with a story that's always good for a laugh when we tell it.

Stories like that are why spending time on the water with Sam is always about more than just fishing.

With 80-plus years on Lake Okeechobee, Sam has plenty of tales about decades past too. They might be about when the lake was filled with gin-clear water and pepper grass or about marsh birds and all the wonders of nature.

Sam's story-telling always has a touch of soft humor in it that makes me laugh and smile.

Part III: The Man, The Myth, The Legend

My wife and I often go down to the South Bay area of the lake to fish. Out in the middle of the bay is this single large wooden pole that we use as a landmark. After a trip down to that area, I was giving Sam a fishing report on our success for the day and asked him about the wooden pole out in the middle of nowhere.

"Sam, we caught a couple good ones by the pole," I said. "What's the name of that pole?"

Sam replied, "The Wonder Pole."

Of course, I asked him why it was called that and he said, "Because everyone wonders why it's there."

Two years ago, we invited Carol and Sam to spend a week with us in Illinois. Sam and I spent our days fishing the backwaters of the Mississippi River and Carol and my wife Mary traveled up and down the area, going to knick-knack shops. The fishing was good for Sam and me, and he showed me that those Florida methods work equally as well on my river.

Sam's topwater fishing skills are second to none. I remember one day when we were fishing dollar pads. I was swimming plastics through the green jungle when Sam picked up his Lil' Richard topwater plug and made a perfect 20-yard cast into a small hole in the pads.

He slowly danced his bait in the hole to entice a bass into striking. As I watched, I wondered how he was going to get that plug with its double set of treble hooks out of that green mess of vegetation.

With a quick flick of his rod tip, he jumped his bait 6 feet and landed it perfectly into the next small opening and continued to work it. With still no takers, he gave his rod tip one more quick flick and landed his bait in the open water next to the boat and made his next cast. I never would have considered using a treble-hook-style bait in such a mass of green, but for Sam, it was never a second thought.

Another day we were out and the wind was blowing about 20 miles per hour, with a good 1 ½-foot chop on the water, even back inside the outer edges of the reeds. I was chuckling and winding my plastics when Sam reached for his topwater plug and started casting to the open water in the heavy chop, away from all the good cover.

I was thinking that Sam must want me to catch all of the fish on this miserable day. But he proceeded to put nine 2-pounders in the boat as I continued to cast to all the good stuff.

Sam also knows how to find fish, especially on Lake Okeechobee. If you have ever fished the lake, you know how it can all start to look the same and how easy it is to get turned around and lost. If it were not for my GPS, I'm sure I would have spent a night or two wandering the marsh, trying to find the boat ramp.

Sam also has a GPS unit in his boat, but he would be the first to tell you that he has no idea how the thing works and, if he did know, he would not trust it.

Sam can get around on the lake better that any man I know and only uses what he calls "Griffin GPS." Sam has mastered the art of triangulation and uses key landmarks to help him move about the lake.

Part III: The Man, The Myth, The Legend

But it is his attention to detail that allows him to return to exactly to same place we were fishing days before. I have been out fishing with Sam when he will say, "Right over there is where we caught that big one."

I can barely remember being in that section of the lake, while he has got it pinned down to a single clump of reeds. I'm still not sure exactly how he is able to zero in on these locations, but Sam is very good at paying attention to the subtle little changes in his surroundings.

He laughs at the comment "it all looks the same." That's because when you look closely, you see ever square foot is different. As Sam constantly reminds me, you just have to look for it. If it were not for me using my GPS and making waypoints on the places where we catch them, I would think he was pulling my leg.

26. What I Learned From Sam About Topwater Lures

By Bernie Schultz

(Like Sam Griffin, Bernie Schultz is a well known Floridian angler. He's an Elite Series pro and a nine-time qualifier for the Bassmaster Classic. Additionally, he's a writer, illustrator and collector of antique fishing tackle.)

Sam and I competed against each other back in 1980s, in the Red Man Tournament Series. I was there when he won on Lake Okeechobee using a topwater of his own design, and he was there when I became top angler in the Gator Division.

As we got to know each other better, I asked him for some custom finishes in my all-time favorites, the "Bass Baffler" and "Jerkin' Sam." Sam not only painted them, he finished some with foil like a Rapala Floating Minnow. I still use them today.

When he stopped turning bodies for Smithwick and started his own venture (the second time), I drew his logo. As a reward, he made me a set of snakeskin baits and presented them on a walnut rack beneath a small glass dome. It's displayed alongside my lure collection to this day. I learned two very important things about topwater lures from Sam. One was the importance of loose hardware … actually loosening the screw eyes and cup spacers so that the props will turn more freely while making a chatter sound. That subtle tip paid off in countless additional fish over my career, and I utilized that very concept in designing the X-Rap Prop by Rapala.

The other lesson was the proper way to tune a propeller. Sam emphasized the importance of securing the flat part around the hole using a pair of pliers, then bending each blade (ear) to the desired angle or pitch with a separate set of pliers. How much bend depends on the sound level and/or the amount of commotion you want the prop/lure to achieve.

Attempting to twist the blades without using pliers results in a bent prop face, which detracts from performance and works against achieving the desired sound levels.

When Sam was on the Glades County Commission, he took action to improve safety on Lake Okeechobee. During his tenure, the lake was lush with tall reeds, many of which grew along narrow channels and kicker trails, forming blind spots in curves and intersections. To help reduce accidents, he had signs installed at key locations like those used on streets and highways.

I enjoyed visiting with Sam at his Moore Haven shop. He was always tinkering with something to fool a bass into striking on the surface.

Sam's a great guy and certainly worthy of recognition. He should be in the (Bass Fishing) Hall of Fame.

27. Sam and the Old Man Pole

(Author's Note: The following was published in the November issue of B.A.S.S. Times. That same month, Sam fell at home and sustained moderate injuries. Fortunately, he recovered quickly. He was back fishing by Christmas and was in fine form when Dave Burkhardt and I made our annual visit in March.)

LAKEPORT, Fla. —At 83, Sam Griffin trailers his boat to Harney Pond Canal access a couple of times a week to go fishing on Lake Okeechobee.

But during recent years, the former guide and longtime lure maker has learned that the blessing of long life brings with it liabilities, and, if he wants to keep fishing, he must make adjustments.

One of those is his self-described "old man pole."

"I put it in about 1 1/2 years ago," he said. "I was going to break off my windshield or bust my butt if I didn't. I needed something more substantial to help me get up and move forward."

To prevent such a mishap, he turned a pedestal seat frame upside down and secured it to both the console and floor. After adding an extension, he sawed off the protruding male end and filled in the opening.

Sam added what he calls an "old man pole" to help him and his fishing companions move about more safely and easily on his boat.

Two friends who recently went fishing with Griffin found the "old man pole" much to their liking as well.

"You don't have to be old to need it," said Floridian Dave Burkhardt. "If someone runs by you and makes a big wave, it's great to hold onto. And it's a huge help for getting on the front deck or stepping down from the back."

Still, Griffin installed it because of what age does to the human body.

"My balance is not what it used to be," he explained. "My brain tells my feet to do something and they don't do it. It preys on your mind. If it's a little choppy, I've actually had to crawl to the bow. It's difficult."

And this loss of mobility and flexibility happens to everyone. One in four Americans 65 and over falls each year, according to the National Council on Aging (NCA). And every 11 seconds, an older adult is treated in the emergency room for a fall, while an older adult dies from a fall every 19 minutes.

"Falls threaten seniors' safety and independence and generate enormous economic and personal costs," the NCA said.

"However, falling is not an inevitable result of aging. Through practical lifestyle adjustments, evidence-based falls prevention programs, and clinical community partnerships, the number of falls among seniors can be substantially reduced."

Lifestyle adjustments in the form of boat modifications, as exemplified by the "old man pole," is exactly what Griffin and thousands of other aging anglers and boat owners are doing annually and what many more should consider if they want to keep spending time on the water. Additionally, these fixes, whether do-it-yourself or after-market products, also can enable those with disabilities unrelated to age to enjoy fishing.

Griffin's second modification, an Easy Step ladder, helps him climb into and out of his boat. The company offers several styles that easily attach to the tongue or frame of a tow trailer.

The Trick Step from Mark Peiser Manufacturing is another popular option. Safety features include handrail, non-skid step pads, and graduated step alignment.

Michigan angler Jeri Toner told B.A.S.S. Times that she "loves" hers.

"I just turned 60, and even though I'm still in decent shape, it's hard getting in and out of my Bass Cat," she said. "Climbing up on the trailer fenders, then hoisting myself over the side of the boat was a chore. Not to mention the occasional slip.

"The Trick Step allows such ease of access. It's mounted at the front side of my trailer. Three easy steps and I'm on the deck of my boat. It makes getting out easy too."

B.A.S.S. Times asked anglers what additional safety/comfort features that they would like to see, not just as add-ons, but as standard on boats, especially for the elderly.

"Emergency ladders should be on all boats," Griffin said. "If you're fishing by yourself and you fall overboard, you could have a serious issue. Or what if someone even older than you falls overboard?"

New Jersey B.A.S.S. member Diane Johnson recommended an "oh, s--t!" rope. She described it as "a knotted rope secured under the passenger's seat for holding on during rough water and waves that can pitch you up and possibly out of your seat."

She added, "I have been in boats that had no side hand-rails or seat straps for passengers to hold onto. Drivers at least have the steering wheel to hold on to."

Meanwhile, Steven Rockweiler of Louisiana suggested that senior anglers would like to see boat manufacturers put the bow eyelet on top instead of the bottom, "where I must get on my hands and knees to unclip my bowline."

He also said that spring-loaded seats would make it easier and safer to elderly anglers to get up and down.

"We're all getting older," Missouri angler Tim Meadows concluded. "Companies need to think about this."

28. Another Nickname

By Larry Penn

My wife and I chose south-central Florida for our retirement primarily for the proximity to Lake Okeechobee and the fishing. When we moved to Lakeport in January 2013, I did not know how fortunate I was to have Sam Griffin as a neighbor. Over the next few years, Sam and I became good friends and fishing buddies. Sam is without a doubt the most knowledgeable person on the lake and in the state of Florida when it comes to fishing and navigating Lake Okeechobee. Most of what I have learned about fishing Lake Okeechobee can be credited to Sam.

Sam has a reputation as the best fisherman on Lake O and, along with that, a number of nicknames, including "the man, the myth, the legend." All are well deserved. But while fishing with me, he acquired another nickname that maybe is not as flattering as the others.

As we were finishing a day's fishing and on the way in to Harney Pond, Sam decided to go to the mouth of Fisheating Creek before calling it a day. The creek can be tricky to get in and out of because of shallow water, swift current, and shifting sandbars. But I had no concerns whatsoever, with my fishing buddy Sam at the controls.

We proceeded toward the creek, cruising about 40 miles per hour with Sam confidently following the channel. Suddenly I looked ahead and saw three or four wading birds standing in the water, with only about 4 to 6 inches of their legs under water. Now far be it for me to tell Sam Griffin which way or where to go, so I just sat there. But I eventually did point towards the birds.

Too Late!

VAAARROOOOM. The outboard flew up out of the water and the boat came to a screeching halt. We were stuck on a sandbar in a heavy Bass Cat bass boat.

We bailed out of the boat and tried to pull it free. But despite our efforts, we couldn't budge the boat even an inch. After a quick call to a local airboat tow service, we were on our way back to the boat dock, lucky to still have a lower unit.

Well it didn't take long for word to get around. The very next day, when Sam went to the local tackle shop for a few things, he was greeted by fishing guides and some of the local hang-arounders with his new nickname.

"Hey, there's Sandbar Sam. How are you doing Sandbar Sam?"

29. A Great Day With Uncle Sam

By Jake Griffin

(Sam Griffin is Jake Griffin's great uncle.)

I have a many good memories of being out on the lake with him.

On one of the earliest times, I wasn't more than 8 or 10 years old. I caught a decent-size bass and remember the rush and excitement of reeling it in, while hearing him giving me reassurance and direction on how to do it.

Another time I went out there with him and my sister Sera. That day we must've caught and released 50 or 60 bass. We used his own lures so we could see how action-packed fishing topwater is. It was a new experience in fishing altogether. He'd tell us to pay attention to the wake coming up to the lure and to determine whether it was a gar or bass. That was one of my and Sera's fondest memories with Uncle Sam, having a great day on the lake.

As I got older, I started to appreciate the wealth of knowledge he had in regard to the lake and to fishing. It was too much to try and absorb all at once, and he simply laughed and said, "Son don't wear yourself out. It takes years of practice."

Big Sam and Big O

We'd had days where we were "outsmarted by those green creatures," as he'd say, but I never left without learning something new, and I cherish those moments.

I'd also vent to him occasionally about my personal life and he always had some easygoing advice that seemed to make things feel better. He knew how to correct my mindset and direct me, when needed.

He is a man of God and a family man. I'm proud to call him "Uncle Sam."

Jake Griffin's son, Dennis, checks out some of the hookless bodies for Uncle Sam's baits.

30. My Friend, Sam Griffin

Sam doesn't turn out as many lures as he used to, and he's retired from guiding. But the man who probably knows more about Lake Okeechobee and its history than any other, still is kind enough to take me fishing annually. I wish that I had kept track of how many years that we have fished together, but I didn't. I do know that my education began in the early 1990s, and I know that Dave Burkhardt and I have visited Sam and Carol annually for more than a decade.

As we fish, Sam shares with Dave and me his knowledge of and love for this natural treasure, as well as the decades of expertise that he has accumulated about topwater fishing specifically and bass fishing generally.

"I love it as much today as when I was 12 and the customers had to crank the boat engine for me," he said.

In turn, I have shared that information about the Big O and bass fishing from Sam in dozens of magazine and online articles for *Bassmaster Magazine*, *B.A.S.S. Times*, and *Bassmaster.com*, as well as other media. (One of those is included in this section of the book.) And I have featured him in my fishing books, *Better Bass Fishing* and *Kickin' Bass*. If you've read either one, you might recognize some of the how-to information from Sam that I've included in this tribute book.

Over the years, other guides, pros, and "experts" have taken me fishing and served as "sources" for me as well. But a trip with Sam is like no other, and, without question, it is one of the highlights of my year—year, after year, after year.

After driving down the night before, our day of fishing starts early, with Sam cooking breakfast for us and then awakening us to feast as he finishes up and sits down to join us in the pre-dawn. Not that I'm complaining, but the menu always had been the same: juice, coffee, scrambled eggs, toast, and turkey bacon.

This past year, though, Sam threw us a curve, and served regular pork bacon. Again, I'm not complaining. When we asked him why, he said that he just got tired of the turkey variety.

Dave and I often tell Sam how much we enjoy those breakfasts. Of course, we do so because they are good, but also because we enjoy the quiet camaraderie of good friends eagerly anticipating what is to come in a shared adventure.

Sam also makes and stores our lunches on his boat for our day of fishing. Those typically are ham and cheese sandwiches, with bananas, some chips and/or crackers, and dessert!

We all have a sweet tooth, it appears. But Sam's seems to be a bit more acute than ours.

For several years, that dessert was honey buns, Sam's favorite. But then the doctor urged him to do something to lower his cholesterol.

Wise man that he is, Sam listened and did something about it. He substituted Twinkies, not exactly known as a health food. During his next visit, the doctor commended him for lowering his cholesterol and, of course, asked him how he did it. Sam eagerly shared his secret—the Twinkie diet!

A trip with Sam is like no other, and, without question, it is one of the highlights of my year.
Photo courtesy of Steve Ulman.

And when he told that story to us one day, as we were eating Twinkies, it immediately became one of my favorite "Sam stories," out of the dozens that he has told us over the years, many of which have nothing to do with fishing. We don't just fish with Sam, we have one heck of a good time doing it. It's a good thing that laughter isn't bad for your cholesterol.

Big Sam and Big O

Finally, I fear that I have tried Sam's patience over the years, as I insist on taking photos of him and Dave, typically with bass that they've just caught. But he never has shown it.

Additionally, he recognized early on that I enjoy photographing wildlife, and he generously has made it his mission to take me to places on the lake where I will have the best opportunities. Because of Sam, I have photographed rare indigo snakes and Everglades kites, as well as spectacular snowy egrets and other bird species too numerous to mention. He's put me up close and personal with manatees and alligators too.

Once we took a long ride to a place that he had spotted otters a few days before. Unfortunately, they no longer were there. But that side trip provided me with the opportunity to photograph one of the largest gators that I've ever seen, as well as green herons, white ibis, and black vultures.

My photo files today are filled with hundreds of wildlife shots that I never could have taken if not for Sam's kindness.

To end my personal tribute to Sam, I'll get back to fishing, and share with you some more of his wisdom, in his own words.

- If you know everything, you'd quit fishing because there's no challenge in it. Every time you go fishing, you think "I'm going to figure this out." But if you did, you wouldn't like that, although you keep trying. That's human nature. Sometimes, you do figure it out, for a given day.
- Tough fishing separates the men from the boys. That's when you have to entice them.

Part III: The Man, The Myth, The Legend

- If you're going to get lost, you want to have a full tank of gas. As long as you have gas, you're never lost.
- When going into a backwater, look behind you so you can see what it looks like when you want to go out.
- I retie every 6 months, whether I need to or not.
- Patience and fishing slowly will catch a lot more fish than fishing fast. I tell people they have to learn to catch more fish rather than make more casts. Be superhumanly patient, and not just when fishing.
- Back when we used to keep fish, I never found wild shiners in a fish unless it was caught on one. More bass eat small to medium baitfish than large baitfish.
- If you want to get a bite, just look away for a second.
- For the last 10 feet to the boat, look at your bait! Watch what's going on in the water when you lift it out. That will help tell you what the fish want.

12/23/20

To, Hannah
and Cameron,
a book to share.
love
O PA

CPSIA information can be obtained
at www.ICGtesting.com
Printed in the USA
LVHW081707071120
671038LV00028B/766